AUDUBON'S BIRDS
OF NORTH AMERICA

Introduction by Sheila Buff

Longmeadow Press

This 1990 edition is published by
Longmeadow Press
201 High Ridge Road
Stamford, CT 06904

ISBN 0-681-40608-9

Publishing Director: Frank Oppel
Editorial Director: Tony Meisel
Design Director: Carmela Pereira
Editor: Theresa Stiles
Composition: Meadowcomp Ltd.
Origination and Printing: Regent Publishing Services Limited

Manufactured in Hong Kong

0 9 8 7 6 5 4 3 2 1

Introduction

The preeminent bird artist of all time—the touchstone for all who came after him—John James Audubon was born Jean Jacques Audubon on 26 April 1785, on his father's sugar plantation in Santo Domingo (now Haiti). His father was Captain Jean Audubon, a French trader, planter, and dealer in slaves; his mother was an obscure Creole woman who died before young Jean Jacques was a year old. Captain Audubon had gone to sea as a boy. In 1770 he started trading in Haiti, and was captain of his own ship by 1774. In 1772 he had married a Frenchwoman, Anne Moynet, who remained behind in France while her husband pursued his business (and other) interests very successfully in the Caribbean. For six years, from 1783 to 1789, Captain Audubon, his son Jean Jacques and a daughter by another Creole woman lived continuously in Haiti. They were reunited with the real Mrs. Audubon in Nantes in 1789. She embraced the two children as her own, and they were eventually legitimized (in 1794) and baptized (in 1800).

Audubon's somewhat murky origins were embarrassing to him. In later life he offered a variety of stories about his birth, occasionally claiming to have been born in Louisiana, or saying that his father had fought with Washington at Valley Forge (where no fighting took place). He also occasionally claimed to be the illegitimate son of King Louis XVI. (This interesting story and other remarks in Audubon's writings later gave rise, in 1937, to a farfetched and tendentious book titled *I Who Should Command All*, which claimed that Audubon was really the Lost Dauphin, son of King Louis XIV and Marie Antoinette. Instead of dying in prison during the French Revolution, the Dauphin was allegedly spirited out of France to America; Audubon was thus supposedly the rightful king of France.)

His wealth notwithstanding, or perhaps because of it, Captain Audubon had become a prominent local leader in the French Revolution. Despite his father's role as a champion of the masses, his son Jean Jacques received the typically bourgeois education of a young man of means, which doubtless included elementary instruction in sketching and draftsmanship. (There is little basis in fact for Audubon's later claim that he studied briefly with the great French neoclassic artist Jacques Louis David.) Young Jean Jacques much preferred to be outdoors, however, and his formal education suffered. Audubon's deep interest in nature came to the surface during his adolescence and coincided with the great resurgence of interest in natural history fostered by French luminaries such as Rousseau, Lamarck, and Buffon.

By 1802 Audubon was seventeen and Napoleon was in power. Young men his age were being drafted into military service, and Captain Audubon wisely decided to send his son to America, both to avoid the draft and to oversee his property there. In early 1804 Jean Jacques arrived in Philadelphia, changed his name to John James, and went to live at his father's estate, Mill Grove. Here the wealthy young man proceeded to live an enjoyable life perfectly suited to his temperament. He wrote of that time, "Hunting, fishing, drawing, music, occupied my every moment; cares I knew not and cared naught about them. I purchased excellent and beautiful horses, visited all such neighbours as I found congenial spirits, and was as happy as happy could be."

Among the neighbors he visited was an Englishman named William Bakewell, who had a charming daughter named Lucy. Audubon began to devote his time to two projects: studying the myriad birds around him and courting Lucy, often simultaneously. By 1804 they were engaged. Audubon's happiness seemed complete, as he wrote of the time, "I had no vices, but was thoughtless, pensive, loving, fond of shooting, fishing, and riding, and had a passion for raising all sorts of fowls, which sources of interest and amusement fully occupied my

3

time. It was one of my fancies to be ridiculously fond of dress; to hunt in black satin breeches, wear pumps when shooting, and to dress in the finest ruffled shirts I could obtain from France."

Interestingly, during this period the pioneering ornithologist Alexander Wilson was living and working in Philadelphia, and indeed that city was the center of natural history studies in America. Audubon apparently had nothing to do with these worthies, and there is no record that he was even aware of their work. At the same time, he was himself making one of the earliest experiments in bird banding by wrapping silver threads around the feet of some baby phoebes he found in a cave. The next year some of the birds returned to the same place.

To the modern reader Audubon's method of studying the birds by shooting them seems appalling. It must be remembered, however, that collecting specimens was standard ornithological practice in the days before high-powered binoculars and color film. Indeed, shooting birds and collecting eggs only ceased to be standard practice toward the end of the nineteenth century. The extensive specimen collections amassed by ornithologists before then, particularly those that contain rare or extinct birds, are still valuable to scientists today, who sometimes must risk arsenic and lead poisoning for the sake of studying them.

Audubon was frustrated in his self-taught efforts to draw the birds in a lifelike manner. Very early one morning, however, insight struck, and he "went off at a gallop towards Norristown. When I arrived there, not a door was open, for it was not yet daylight. I went to the river, took a bath and returning to the town inquired for wire of different sizes, bought some and was soon again at Mill Grove. I shot the first kingfisher I met, pierced the body with a wire, fixed it to the board, another wire held the head, smaller ones fixed the feet. The last wire proved a delightful elevator to the bird's tail and at last--there stood before me the real kingfisher. I outlined this bird, colored it. This was my first drawing actually from nature." Later, Audubon refined this technique by placing the bird against a background grid and by using calipers to take careful measurements.

Early in 1805 Audubon strongly disagreed with his father's agent, a man who had been sent over to help Audubon mine the lead ore that had been found on his property. Audubon returned to France to see his family, straighten out his business ventures, and get his father's permission to marry Lucy. While in France he formed, with his father's assistance, a business partnership with a young man about his age named Ferdinand Rozier. They returned to Philadelphia in 1806 to operate the lead mine. Once back at Mill Grove, however, Audubon quickly forgot about the lead mine and began devoting himself more single-mindedly to bird studies. William Bakewell, Lucy's brother, described Audubon at the time: "Audubon took me to his house, where he and his companion, Rozier, resided, with Mrs. Thomas for an attendant. On entering his room, I was astonished and delighted that it was turned into a museum. The walls were festooned with all sorts of birds' eggs, carefully blown out and strung on a thread. The chimney piece was covered with stuffed squirrels, raccoons and opossums; and the shelves around were likewise crowded with specimens, among which were fishes, frogs, snakes, lizards, and other reptiles. Besides these stuffed varieties, many paintings were arrayed upon the walls, chiefly of birds. He had great skill in stuffing and preserving animals of all sorts. He had also a trick of training dogs with great perfection, of which art his famous dog Zephyr was a wonderful example. He was an admirable marksman, an expert swimmer, a clever rider, possessed of great activity, prodigious strength, and was notable for the elegance of his figure, and the beauty of his features, and he aided Nature by a careful attendance to his dress. Besides other accomplishments, he was musical, a good fencer, danced well, had some acquaintance with legerdemain tricks, worked in hair, and could plait willow baskets." This formidable list of accomplishments did not, alas, include a talent for business. Audubon and Rozier failed as lead miners, and the Audubon interest in Mill Grove was sold. Rozier joined a firm of Philadelphia merchants, and Audubon became a clerk to Lucy's uncle Benjamin Bakewell, a merchant in New York City. Preoccupied with birds, far from Lucy, and bored by the counting house, Audubon was, to put it charitably, a hopeless failure at business. A telling anecdote about him from this period claims that he once mailed off eight thousand dollars in an unsealed envelope. Audubon's companion and erstwhile partner Rozier was doing no better in Philadelphia. Surprisingly, in view of their decidedly mixed business experience, the two decided to use the proceeds from the sale of Mill Grove to open a general store in Louisville, Kentucky. This decision is not as inexplicable as it seems at first. Kentucky was then the frontier, a place where young men with more drive than bookkeeping skills could be successful entrepreneurs and still have lots of time for hunting, fishing, and other engaging pursuits. In 1807 Rozier and Audubon set up shop. In the spring of 1808 Audubon came back to Philadelphia, married Lucy, and returned to Louisville with her.

Audubon was no more practical than before. While Rozier minded the shop, he roamed the countryside, fishing, hunting, and studying and drawing the birds. In March of 1810 Audubon met Alexander Wilson, an chance encounter that had important repercussions. According to Audubon's account of the meeting, "One fair morning I was surprised by the sudden entrance into our counting room at Louisville of Mr. Alexander Wilson, the celebrated author of the American Ornithology, of whose existence I had never until that moment been apprised. . . . He had two volumes under his arm, and as he approached the table at which I was working, I thought I discovered something like astonishment in his countenance. He, however, immediately proceeded to disclose the object of his visit, which was to procure subscriptions for his work. He opened his books, explained the nature of his occupation, and requested my patronage. I felt surprised and gratified at the sight of his volumes, turned over a few of the plates, and had already taken my pen to write my name in his favour, when my partner said rather abruptly to me in French: "My dear Audubon, what induces you to subscribe to this work? Your drawings are certainly far better; and again, you must know as much of the habits of American birds as this gentleman.' Whether Mr. Wilson understood French or not, or if the suddenness with which I paused disappointed him, I cannot tell; but I clearly perceived he was not pleased. Vanity, and the encomiums of my friend, prevented me from subscribing. Mr. Wilson asked me if I had many drawings of birds. I rose, took down a large portfolio, laid it on the table, and showed him as I would show you, kind reader, or any other person fond of such subjects, the whole of the contents, with the same patience, with which he had showed me his own engravings. His surprise appeared great, as he told me he had never had the most distant idea that any other individual than himself had been engaged in forming such a collection. He asked me if it was my intention to publish, and when I answered in the negative, his surprise seemed to increase. And, truly, such was not my intention; for, until long after, when I met the Prince of Musignano in Philadelphia, I had not the least idea of presenting the fruits of my labours to the world. Mr. Wilson now examined my drawings with care, asked if I should have any objections to lending him a few during his stay, to which I replied that I had none. He then bade me good morning, not, however, until I had made an arrangement to explore the woods in the vicinity with him, and had promised to procure for him some birds, of which I had drawings in my collection, but which he had never seen. . . .

"We hunted together and obtained birds which he had never before seen; but, reader, I did not subscribe to his work, for, even at that time, my collection was greater than his."

In contrast to the ebullient Audubon's lengthy account, the dour Wilson's diary is oddly laconic. He wrote, "Rambled around the town with my gun. Examined Mr. [Audubon's] drawings in crayon—very good."

The firm of Rozier and Audubon soon ran into an unanticipated obstacle: competition. Other stores in Louisville were run on more businesslike lines, and in spring of 1810 the partners loaded their stock and household goods onto a flatboat and, leaving Lucy behind, drifted down the Ohio River some 125 miles to Henderson, Kentucky. From there they pushed onward to the village of Ste. Genevieve on the Mississippi and set up shop. Audubon realized that life in Ste. Genevieve would be far too raw for Lucy. He dissolved his partnership with Rozier and returned to Henderson, where he began a new business with Lucy's brother Thomas. (Rozier, without the burden of his partner, apparently went on to be quite successful as a shopkeeper.) Audubon stayed with it for the next seven years, achieving some moderate success even though he spent much of time hunting or drawing birds, sometimes in the company of his friend Daniel Boone. Whatever money Audubon made from the general store, however, he managed to lose in a series of terrible investments. By 1819 he was in jail for debt. Of this time Audubon wrote, "I parted with every particle of property I had to my creditors, keeping only the clothes I wore on that day, my original drawings, and my gun, and without a dollar in my pocket, walked to Louisville alone." The journey at this low ebb, he wrote, was "the only time in my life when the wild turkeys that so often crossed my path, and the thousands of lesser birds that enlivened the woods and the prairies, all looked like enemies, and I turned my eyes from them, as if I could have wished that they had never existed."

Basically an optimistic sort, Audubon soon bounced back from his depression. Always a good draftsman, he set up as an itinerant portrait painter, writing, "As we were straightened to the very utmost, I undertook to draw portraits at the low price of five dollars per head, in black chalk. I drew a few gratis, and succeeded so well that ere many days had elapsed I had an abundance of work."

In the days before photography, the traveling portrait artist could always find work of a sort—even if it meant painting a sign or two as part of the deal. Audubon was soon back on his feet and living in a house in Louisville, but was also soon busier painting portraits of birds than people.

An opportunity well suited to Audubon's peculiar mix of talents arose in 1820: the post of taxidermist at the Western Museum in Cincinnati. His duties at the museum were not particularly pressing, and Audubon still had plenty of time to pursue his avian interests. The museum's head, Dr. Daniel Drake (himself a fairly colorful frontier character), introduced Audubon to the naturalists who came to visit the museum. Among them were Titian Ramsey Peale, son of the artist Charles Peale and himself a noted artist (he was, among other accomplishments, the official artist of the famous around-the-world United States Exploring Expedition of 1838-42). The visitors were shown Audubon's paintings, and most were deeply impressed. The positive reception Audubon received convince him to publish his work.

To that end, Audubon decided to undertake a systematic survey of the country southwest of the Mississippi. In October of 1820, leaving Lucy and his children behind in Cincinnati, he headed down the river to collect and paint birds, paying his way by painting portraits. He landed in New Orleans, where he continued to paint portraits and gave private lessons in drawing. Lucy joined him, and eventually found a position as a sort of governess/ schoolteacher at a small school on a plantation called Beech Woods, outside New Orleans.

By the fall of 1823 Audubon felt ready to attempt publication of his bird paintings. He left for Philadelphia, still the bastion of natural history, arriving there in April of 1824. Audubon here encountered both opposition--from George Ord, Alexander Wilson's disciple—and encouragement—from Charles Lucien Bonaparte, nephew of Napoleon and a leading ornithologist in his own right. The disapprovers outnumbered the approvers, however, and Audubon gave up on publishing in Philadelphia. In August he arrived in New York City with the same goal, but again could find no publisher to take on the project. Disconsolate, he returned to Lucy at Beech Woods. Here he instructed the students in French, music, and drawing, and continued to paint the birds. He and Lucy worked hard and saved their money, always with the goal of publication in front of them. Lucy's dedication to her wandering (and occasionally philandering) husband was remarkable. Audubon wrote of this time, "My best friends solemnly regarded me as a mad man, and my wife and family alone gave me encouragement. My wife determined that my genius should prevail, and that my final success as an ornithologist should be triumphant."

In April of 1826 Audubon again left Lucy to search for a publisher, this time in England. Arriving in Liverpool in July, he called on friends of a friend and presented his letter of introduction. He was warmly welcomed into the wealthy, cultivated, and friendly William Rathbone family. The Rathbones were well connected among natural history circles in England, and offered to be Audubon's first subscribers. The combination of Audubon's romantic good looks, undeniable charm, exotic experiences as an American woodsman, and enormous artistic talent quickly made him into an overnight success. Within a few days of his arrival, Audubon found his paintings on display at the Royal Institution in Liverpool, where the admission fees of a shilling a head quickly amounted to a hundred pounds.

Despite his success, however, Audubon still could not find a publisher. His quest next took him to Edinburgh, then a center of scientific activity. Here Audubon made a deep impression on the resident sages, and was elected a fellow of the Royal Society in Edinburgh. He brought his portfolio to William Lizars, considered the finest engraver in all of Scotland. Lizars, deeply impressed, agreed to engrave the drawings. He and Audubon drew up a prospectus for the work, deciding to call it *The Birds of America*. Lizars would engrave each of four hundred of Audubon's bird drawings, to be printed life-size on the large paper known as double elephant; the engravings would be colored by hand. There would be one drawing per plate, and five plates per folio, or part. Five parts, or twenty-five plates, would be issued each year until all the plates were published; the cost per part was two guineas (roughly twelve dollars at the time). To make the venture profitable, three hundred subscribers were needed.

Audubon now embarked on the wearying quest for subscribers, armed only with the prospectus and a single sample plate. Cutting his long hair and giving up his quaint frontier costume, Audubon headed toward London, stopping in various cities along the way to collect names on his subscription list. Arriving in London in the spring of 1827, Audubon received bad news from Lizars. The engraving was going not at all well. Only ten plates were ready, and it was all costing a good deal more than estimated.

Audubon moved with somewhat uncharacteristic haste and firmness. He removed the work from Lizars and turned it over to a talented young engraver in London, Robert Havell, Jr. Young Havell was particularly skilled in the art of the aquatint, which had been invented around 1780. This method of etching uses a plate of polished copper or zinc coated with a thin layer of grainy resin. The engraver copies the original directly onto the plate (usually by tracing), cutting through the resin into the metal, and then places the plate into an acid bath. The acid cuts into the plate, but does not penetrate the grains of resin. The resulting lines thus present a broken, not solid, appearance, very like a watercolor. Indeed, after Havell's prints of Audubon's birds were carefully hand-colored, they were virtually indistinguishable from an original watercolor at all but close distance.

The question of engraver now settled for good (Havell would produce all 435 engravings for *The Birds of America* over the next eleven years), Audubon concentrated on the discouraging job of corralling subscribers. The task was eased somewhat when the dyspeptic King George IV unexpectedly agreed to meet Audubon and become a subscriber.

By 1828 Audubon had some seventy subscribers in England and Scotland, and decided to try his luck in Paris. Here he garnered a dozen or so more subscriptions, and received the praise of numerous artists and naturalists.

Feeling perhaps that he had saturated the market for the time being, Audubon left Havell with enough drawings to keep him busy for a year and sailed back to New Orleans in 1829. He arrived in November, and by the first of the new year he, along with Lucy and their son John, returned to England. On the way they stopped in Washington, D.C., and were received by President Andrew Jackson, and where the Library of Congress subscribed to *The Birds of America*. In 1830 his reputation was further enhanced when he was elected a Fellow of the Royal Society in London.

Temporarily settled in Edinburgh, Audubon began to work on the next step in his undertaking: an explanatory text, called *Ornithological Biography*, to accompany the engravings. In this effort Audubon had the good fortune to be assisted by the Scottish naturalist Alexander MacGillivray. As a writer Audubon tended toward hyperbole and shaky grammar; MacGillivray acted as editor. Intended to be strictly scientific, but based on Audubon's journals and observations, the text imperceptibly and delightfully came to include information and anecdotes about Audubon's own adventurous life. Audubon and MacGillivray, assisted by Lucy, worked diligently, spurred by the knowledge that Alexander Wilson was planning to publish his *American Ornithology* in Edinburgh soon. Audubon wanted to get his book out before Wilson published his, but could find no publisher in Edinburgh willing to take on the job. He ended up publishing it at his own expense in March of 1831 at which time it was well received.

By the summer of 1831 the first volume of *The Birds of America* was complete, after four years of toil and anxiety. Audubon decided to return to America for another bird-collecting expedition. He brought with him a well-established European reputation, one that finally impressed the worthies of Philadelphia. A subscription came from the Philadelphia Academy of Natural Sciences.

Audubon headed to Charleston, where he had a chance meeting with the Reverend John Bachman. A man of the cloth but also a well-known naturalist, Bachman immediately became a lifelong, close friend of Audubon. So close were the two families that Audubon's sons, John and Victor, eventually married Bachman's two eldest daughters.

In search of southern birds, Audubon went on to Florida for the winter of 1831-2, but was disappointed both by the country and the birds he saw there. In the summer of 1832 he and his family made a leisurely birding trip to Maine and New Brunswick. By the fall they were all in Boston. Audubon sent Victor off to London to supervise Havell and drum up sales, while he stayed in America, working on his drawings (assisted by John) and planning an expedition to Labrador.

Audubon's Labrador trip began in the early spring of 1833 and lasted until the end of the summer. He collected seventy-three new specimens and made many drawings, as well as keeping a journal that contains some of his most eloquent writing. (Actually, Audubon kept journals more or less continuously throughout his life, and they are a major source of information about him. However, most of the journals were heavily edited and censored by Lucy and his granddaughter Maria, and are thus a major source of distortion.)

Audubon spent most of the winter of 1833-4 in Charleston with the Bachman family. Then he was off to London with Lucy and John in April, where they found Victor doing well and the business of publication proceeding prosperously. In the fall he traveled to Edinburgh, where he spent the next eighteen months working with MacGillivray on the second and third volumes of the *Ornithological Biography*. With the major part of this work now behind him, Audubon embarked on a new series of travels, including another visit to Charleston. Sometime in the winter of 1836-7, he and Bachman conceived the idea of a new book to be called *Quadrupeds of North America* and began some preliminary work on it. Later in 1837 Audubon explored the Gulf of Mexico and Texas. The result was that he now wanted to add eighty-seven species to *the Birds of America*. The problem was in asking the subscribers to pay for the additional plates. To get around the problem, Audubon began putting several different birds into one plate.

By now the great work was drawing to a close. On 20 June 1838 the final plate of *The Birds of America* was engraved; in May of the next year the fifth and final volume of the *Ornithological Biography* was complete. In total, *The Birds of America* contains 435 plates illustrating 1,055 specimens of 489 species. The work in its final form consists of four volumes, each more than three feet long, over two feet wide, and very heavy. There is no exact figure for the number of sets printed; expert estimates range from 161 to 175. Of the sets printed, about a hundred were sold in England and Scotland, a few were sold in Continental Europe, and most of the rest were sold in America. Interestingly, because production expenses were so high, Audubon probably made more money from the *Ornithological Biography* than he did from the original *Birds of America*.

What made *The Birds of America* truly profitable to Audubon was a smaller and more manageable edition published in royal octavo size. This edition was lithographed (instead of engraved) and hand-colored by J.T. Bowen of Philadelphia and was issued in a hundred parts of five plates each; in total the work came to seven volumes. It differed from the double elephant folios in grouping the birds by species and devoting a separate plate to every species. Some new species recently discovered in the West were also added. This edition was the basis for the beautiful later editions, including the present one, that were printed in color instead of being hand-colored. The original double elephant folio would have cost an American subscriber one thousand dollars; in 1989, one of these folios was sold at auction for almost four million dollars.

Audubon plunged immediately into work on *The Quadrupeds of North America*, assisted by Bachman, John, and Victor. In the spring of 1843 he went on his last long journey, an eight-month trek to the Yellowstone River and back. The work was based on 150 folio drawings by Audubon and his sons, lithographed and hand-colored by J.T. Bowen. The first volume of *The Quadrupeds* was published in 1845; the remaining volumes of illustration and text were mainly the work of Victor and John, and were published by 1848. By then, Audubon was slowly losing his mental faculties, although he was never physically ill. He had retired to the home he purchased in 1841 just north of Manhattan (now Audubon Park in the Bronx, one of the few places he stayed in long enough during his itinerant life to be named for him), where he lived quietly with Lucy until his death on 27 January 1851, at the age of 76.

Audubon's artistic legacy lives on, of course, but not only in the many popular editions of his work. His name today is synonymous with the combination of artistic and scientific integrity. His love of the wilderness and care for living things is memorialized by the National Audubon Society and the various state Audubon Societies—organizations founded at the turn of the twentieth century to preserve and protect the natural places and creatures that Audubon brought to the world so vividly in his art.

Sheila Buff
Red Hook, New York

Plate 1

Californian Turkey Vulture.

Drawn from Nature by J.J.Audubon, F.R.S.F.L.S.   Lith. Printed & Col.ᵈ by J.T.Bowen, Phil.ᵃ

Pl. 2

Red-headed Turkey Vulture.

Drawn from Nature by J.J.Audubon, F.R.S.F.L.S   Lith. Printed & Col.d by J.T. Bowen, Phil

Pl. 3.

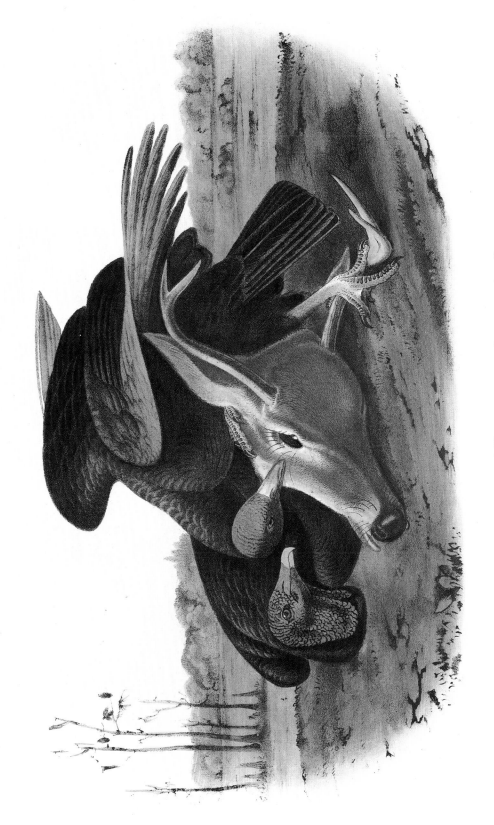

Black Vulture or Carrion Crow.

Drawn from Nature by J.J.Audubon, F.R.S.F.L.S.

Pl. 4.

Caracara Eagle.

Drawn from Nature by J.J.Audubon, F.R.S.F.L.S.   Lith. Printed & Col.d by J.T. Bowen, Phila.

Pl. 5

Harris's Buzzard

Drawn from Nature by J.J.Audubon, F.R.S.F.L.S.

Lith.Printed & Col.d by J.T.Bowen, Phila.

Pl. 6.

Common Buzzard

Drawn from Nature by J.J.Audubon,F.R.S.F.L.S.   Lith⁴Printed & Col⁴by J. T Bowen Philad⁴

Pl. 7.

Red-tailed Buzzard.

Drawn from Nature by J.J.Audubon,F.R.S.F.L.S.   Lith.ᵈPrinted & Col.ᵈby J.T.Bowen,Philad.ᵃ

15

Pl. 8.

Harlan's Buzzard.

Drawn from Nature by J.J.Audubon.F.R.S.F.L.S.   Lith.ᵈ Printed & Col.ᵈ by J. T. Bowen, Philadᵃ

Pl. 9.

Red-shouldered Buzzard.

Drawn from Nature by J.J.Audubon, F.R.S.F.L.S.   Lith.^d Printed & Col.^d by J.T.Bowen, Philad.^a

Pl 10

Broad winged Buzzard

Drawn from Nature by J.J Audubon, F.R.S.F.L.S.

Lith⁴ Printed & Col⁴ by J. T. Bowen Philad⁴

Pl. 11.

Rough-legged Buzzard.

Drawn from Nature by J.J.Audubon,FRSFLS.

Lith⁴Printed & Col⁴by J. T. Bowen, Philad⁴

Golden Eagle.

Drawn from Nature by J.J.Audubon.F.R.S.F.L.S.   Lith⁴ Printed & Col⁴ by J.T Bowen, Philad⁴

Pl. 13.

Washington Sea Eagle.

Drawn from Nature by J.J.Audubon. F.R.S.F.L.S.   Lith.d Printed & Col.d by J. T. Bowen. Philad.

Pl. 14

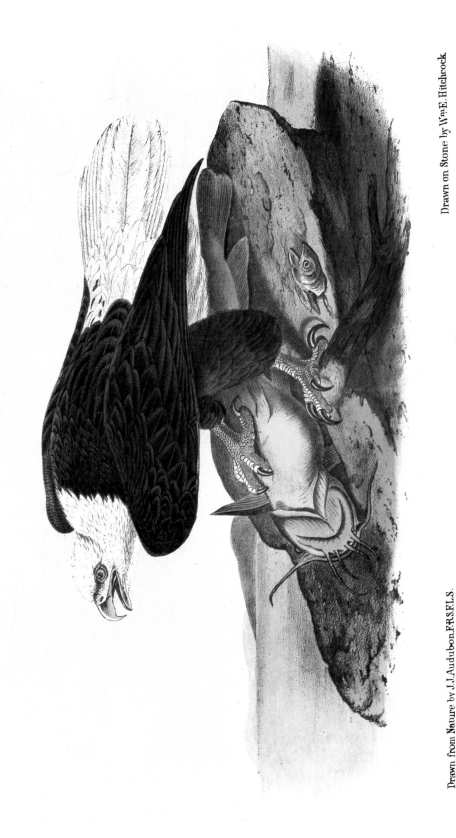

Drawn from Nature by J.J.Audubon.F.R.S.F.L.S.

Drawn on Stone by Wⁿᵉ E. Hitchcock

White-headed Sea-Eagle or Bald-Eagle

Pl. 15.

Common Osprey Fish Hawk.

Drawn from Nature by J.J.Audubon, FRS.FLS.   Lith. Printed & Col.ᵈ by J.T.Bowen, Phila.

Pl. 16.

Black-shouldered Elanus.

Drawn from nature by J. W. Audubon.   Lith. & col. by Bowen & Co. Philad ᵃ

Pl. 17.

Drawn from Nature by J.J.Audubon,F.R.S.F.L.S.   Lith.ᵈ Printed & Col.ᵈ by J. T. Bowen, Philad.ᵈ

Mississipi Kite.

Pl. 18.

Drawn from Nature by J.J.Audubon, F.R.S.F.L.S.

Lith.ᵈ Printed & Col.ᵈ by J.T.Bowen, Philad.ᵃ

Swallow-tailed Hawk.

26

Pl. 19.

Drawn from Nature by J.J.Audubon,F.R.S.F.L.S.   Lith.ᵈ Printed & Col.ᵈ by J.T.Bowen,Philad.

Iceland or Gyr Falcon

Pl. 20.

Drawn from Nature by J.J.Audubon, F.R.S.F.L.S.

Lith. & Col. Bowen & Co Philad.ª

Peregrine Falcon.

28

Pl. 21.

Pigeon Falcon.

Drawn from Nature by J.J.Audubon, F.R.S.F.L.S.

Lith.^d Printed & Col.^d by J. T. Bowen, Philad.^a

Pl. 22.

Sparrow Falcon.

Drawn from Nature by J.J.Audubon,FRSFLS

Lith⁴ Printed & Col⁴ by J T Bowen, Philad⁴

Pl. 23.

Gos Hawk.

Drawn from Nature by J.J.Audubon,F.R.S.F.L.S.

31

Lith⁴ Printed & Col⁴ by J T Bowen, Philad⁴

Pl. 24.

Cooper's Hawk

Drawn from Nature by J.J.Audubon,FRS.FLS.

Lith⁴Printed & Col⁴by J. T Bowen, Philad⁴

Pl. 25.

Sharp-shinned Hawk.

Drawn from Nature by J.J.Audubon,FRSFLS.   Lith⁴Printed & Col⁴by J.T.Bowen Philad

Pl. 26.

Common Harrier.

Drawn from Nature by J.J.Audubon.FRSFLS.   Lith⁴ Printed & Col⁴ by J. T. Bowen. Philad⁴

Pl. 27.

Hawk Owl.

Drawn from Nature by J.J.Audubon,FRSFLS._   Lith⁴ Printed & Col⁴ by J.T.Bowen, Philad⁴

Pl. 28

Snowy Owl.

Drawn from Nature by J.J.Audubon,F.R.S.F.L.S.   Lith'd Printed & Col'd by J. T. Bowen, Philad.

Pl. 29.

Passerine Day-Owl

Drawn from Nature by J.J.Audubon,F.R.S.F.L.S.

37

Lith⁴ Printed & Col⁴ by J.T.Bowen, Philad⁴

Pl. 30.

Columbian Day-Owl.

Drawn from Nature by J.J.Audubon,F.R.S.FL.S.   Lith.Printed & Col.d by J.T.Bowen,Philad.a

Pl. 31.

Drawn from Nature by J J Audubon. F.R.S.F.L.S.

Burrowing Day-Owl.

Lith. Printed & Col⁴ by J.T.Bowen, Philad⁴.

Pl. 32.

Tengmalms Night-Owl.

Drawn from Nature by J.J.Audubon,F.R.S.F.L.S Lith⁴ Printed & Col⁴ by J T Bowen Philad⁴

Pl. 33.

Little or Acadian Owl

Common Mouse

Drawn from Nature by J.J.Audubon,F.R.S.F.L.S.   Lith⁴ Printed & Col⁴ by J.T.Bowen, Philad⁴

Pl 34

Barn Owl

Drawn from Nature by JJ Audubon, FRSFLS   Lith. & Col. Bowen & Co. Philad.ᵃ

Pl. 35.

Great Cinereous Owl.

Drawn from Nature by J.J. Audubon. F.R.S.F.L.S.

Lith.d Printed & Col.d by J.T. Bowen, Philada.

43

Pl. 36.

Barred Owl.

Drawn from Nature by J.J.Audubon,FRS.FLS.   Lith.d Printed & Col.d by J T Bowen Philad.a

44

Pl. 37.

Long-eared Owl.

Drawn from Nature by J.J.Audubon,F.R.S.F.L.S.   Lith⁴ Printed & Col⁴ by J.T.Bowen. Philād⁴

45

Pl. 38.

Drawn from Nature by J.J.Audubon F.R.S.F.L.S.

Short-eared Owl.

Lith Printed & Col.ᵈ by J.T.Bowen, Philad.ᵃ

Pl. 39.

Great Horned-Owl.

Drawn from Nature by J.J.Audubon,F.R.S.F.L.S.

Lith⁴ Printed & Col⁴ by J. T. Bowen, Philad⁴

47

Pl.40.

Little Screech Owl.

Jersey Pine. Pinus inops.

Drawn from Nature by J.J.Audubon,F.R.S.F.L.S.   Lith⁴Printed & Col⁴by J.T.Bowen,Philad⁴

Pl 41

Chuck-will's Widow.
(Harlequin Snake.)

Drawn from Nature by J.J.Audubon,F.R.S.F.L.S.　　　Lith⁴Printed & Col⁴by J.T.Bowen Philad

Pl. 42

Whip-poor-will

Black Oak or Quercitron. Quercus tinctoria.

Drawn from Nature by J.J.Audubon,F.R.S.F.L.S. 50 Lith⁴ Printed & Col⁴ by J.T.Bowen Phila.

Pl. 43.

Night Hawk

White Oak Quercus Alba

Drawn from Nature by J.J.Audubon,F.R.S.F.L.S.

51

Lith⁴Printed & Col⁴by J.T.Bowen,Philad⁴

Pl.44.

American Swift

(Nests.)

Drawn from Nature by J.J.Audubon.FRS.FLS

52

Lith.d Printed & Col.d by J.T Bowen, Philad.a

Pl. 45

Purple Martin.

(Calabash.)

Drawn from Nature by J.J.Audubon,F.R.S.F.L.S

Lith⁴Printed & Col⁴by J T.Bowen, Philad⁴

Pl 46.

White-bellied Swallow.

Drawn from Nature by J.J.Audubon.FRS.FLS.   Lith⁴ Printed & Col⁴ by J T Bowen Philad⁴

54

Pl. 47

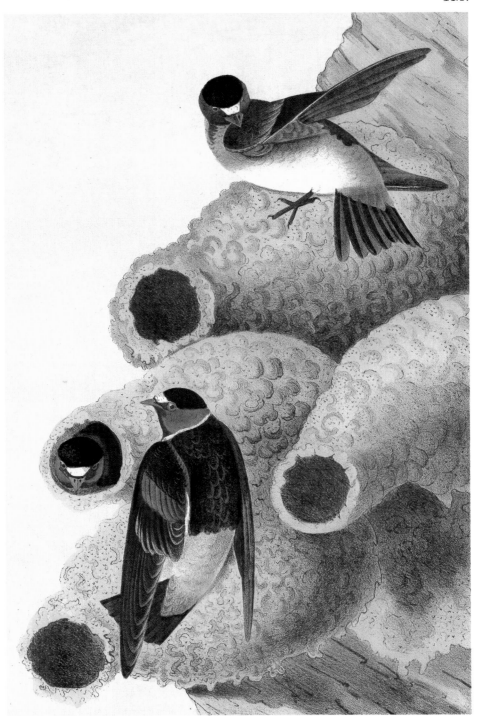

Cliff Swallow.

(Nests.)

Drawn from Nature by J.J.Audubon,F.R.S.F.L.S

Lith⁴ Printed & Col⁴ by J. T. Bowen Philad⁴

Pl. 48.

Barn or Chimney Swallow

Drawn from Nature by J.J.Audubon,F.R.S.F.L.S.　　　　　　Lith⁴ Printed & Col⁴ by J. T Bowen Philad⁴

Plate 49.

Violet Green Swallow

Drawn from Nature by J.J.Audubon,F.R.S.F.L.S.   Lith, Printed & Col.ᵈ by J. T. Bowen, Phil.ᵃ

Pl. 50

Bank Swallow

Drawn from Nature by J.J.Audubon,FRSFLS.   Lith⁴ Printed & Col⁴ by J T Bowen Phil.ad

Pl. 51.

Rough-winged Swallow.

Drawn from Nature by J.J.Audubon,FRSFLS.   Lith⁴Printed & Col⁴by J.T.Bowen,Philad⁴

Pl. 52

Fork tailed Flycatcher.
Gordonia Lasianthus.

Drawn from Nature by J.J.Audubon,F.R.S.FL.S.   Lith^{d} Printed & Col^{d} by J T Bowen Philad^{a}

60

Pl 53

Swallow-tailed Flycatcher.

Drawn from Nature by J.J.Audubon,FRSFLS.   Lith\.P\. \.ed & Col\.by J.T.Bowen Ph\.\.\.\.

Pl. 54.

Arkansas Flycatcher.

Drawn from Nature by J.J.Audubon, F.R.S.F.L.S.

Lith.ᵈ Printed & Col.ᵈ by J. T. Bowen, Philad.ᵈ

Pl.55.

Pipiry Flycatcher
Agati Grandiflora

Drawn from Nature by J.J.Audubon,F.R.S.F.L.S.   Lith⁴ Printed & Col⁴ by J. T. Bowen, Phlad

Pl. 56.

Tyrant Flycatcher or King Bird.

Cotton wood Populus candicans.

Drawn from Nature by J.J.Audubon,F.R.S.F.L.S.   Lith⁴ Printed & Col⁴ by J.T.Bowen, Philad⁴

Pl. 57.

Great Crested Flycatcher.

Drawn from Nature by J.J.Audubon,F.R.S.F.L.S.   Lit. Printed & Col.d by J. T. Bowen, Philad.a

Pl. 58.

Cooper's Flycatcher.

(Balsam or Silver Fir. Pinus Balsamea.)

Male 1. Female 2.

Drawn from Nature by J.J.Audubon.FRSFLS.

Lith.d Printed & Col.d by J.T.Bowen, Philad.a

Pl. 59

Say's Flycatcher

1. Male 2. Female.

Drawn from Nature by J.J.Audubon,F.R.S.F.L.S.

Lith.ᵈ Printed & Col.ᵈ by J. T. Bowen, Philad.ᵃ

67

Pl. 60.

Rocky Mountain Flycatcher.
(*Swamp Oak Quercus Aquatica.*)
Male.

Drawn from Nature by J.J.Audubon,F.R.S.F.L.S.   Lith.ᵈ Printed & Col.ᵈ by J. T. Bowen, Philad.ᵈ

Pl. 61

Short-legged Pewit Flycatcher
(Hobble Bush Viburnum Lantanerdes.)
Male.

Drawn from Nature by J.J.Audubon,F.R.S.F.L.S. Lith.ᵈPrinted & Col.ᵈby J. T. Bowen.Plulad.

Pl. 62

Small Green-crested Flycatcher.

Sassafras Laurus Sassafras.

1. Male 2. Female

Drawn from Nature by J.J.Audubon,F.R.S.F.L.S. 70 Lith.d Printed & Col.d by J. T. Bowen, Philad.a

Pl. 63

Pewee Flycatcher.

Cotton Plant. Gossypium. Herbaceum.

1. Male 2. Female.

Drawn from Nature by J.J.Audubon, F.R.S.F.L.S.

71

Lith.^d Printed & Col.^d by J. T. Bowen, Philad.^a

Pl. 64.

Wood Pewee Flycatcher

Swamp Honeysuckle. Azalea Viscosa

Male.

Drawn from Nature by J.J.Audubon,F.R.S.F.L.S.　　　　　Lithd Printed & Cold by J. T. Bowen, Philad.a

Pl. 65.

Drawn from Nature by J.J.Audubon,F.R.S.F.L.S

Lith.ᵈ Printed & Col.ᵈ by J. T. Bowen, Philad.ᵃ

Traill's Flycatcher.
Male.
Sweet Gum. Liquidambar Styracifolia.

Pl. 66.

Least Pewee Flycatcher?

White Oak. Quercus Prinus.

Male.

Drawn from Nature by J.J.Audubon,F.R.S.F.L.S.

Lith.d Printed & Col.d by J.T.Bowen, Philad.a

Pl. 67.

Small-headed Flycatcher

Virginian Spider-wort. Tradescantia Virginica.

Male.

Drawn from Nature by J.J.Audubon,F.R.S.F.L.S.

Lith⁴Printed & Col⁴by J.T.Bowen, Philad⁴

75

Pl. 68.

American Redstart

Virginian Hornbeam or Iron-wood Tree.

1. Male 2. Female.

Drawn from Nature by J.J.Audubon,F.R.S.F.L.S.

76

Lith⁴ Printed & Col⁴ by J.T.Bowen, Phil⁴ᵃ

Pl. 69.

Townsend's Ptilogonys.

Female.

Drawn from Nature by J.J.Audubon,F.R.S.F.L.S.

Lith⁴ Printed & Col⁴ by J.T.Bowen, Philad⁴

77

Pl. 70.

Blue-grey Flycatcher

Black Walnut Juglans nigra

1 Male 2. Female.

Drawn from Nature by J.J.Audubon,F.R.S.F.L.S. Lith.d Printed & Col.d by J.T.Bowen, Philad.a

Pl. 71.

Hooded Flycatching Warbler.

Erithryna herbacea.

1. Male 2. Female.

Drawn from Nature by J.J.Audubon, F.R.S.F.L.S.

Lith.ᵈ Printed & Col.ᵈ by J T Bowen, Philad.

Pl. 72

Canada Flycatcher.

Great Laurel Rhododendron maximum.

1. Male. 2. Female.

Drawn from Nature by J.J.Audubon,F.R.S.F.L.S.

80

Lith⁴ Printed & Col⁴ by J. T. Bowen, Phila⁴ˢ

Pl. 73.

Bonapartes Flycatching-Warbler.

Great Magnolia. Magnolia Grandiflora.

Male.

Drawn from Nature by J.J.Audubon,F.R.S.F.L.S.

81

Lith⁴Printed & Col⁴by J.T.Bowen,Philad⁴

Pl. 74.

Kentucky Flycatching Warbler.

Magnolia auriculata.

1. Male. 2. Female.

Drawn from Nature by J.J.Audubon, F.R.S.F.L.S.　　　Lith.ᵈ Printed & Col.ᵈ by J. T. Bowen, Philad.ᵃ

Pl. 75.

Wilson's Flycatching-Warbler.

Snake's Head Chelone Glabra.

1. Male 2. Female.

Drawn from Nature by J.J.Audubon,F.R.S.F.L.S.

83

Lith⁴ Printed & Col⁴ by J.T.Bowen, Philad⁴

Pl. 76.

Yellow-crowned Wood-Warbler.

Iris versicolor.

1. Male. 2. Young.

Drawn from Nature by J.J.Audubon.F.R.S.F.L.S.

Lith.ᵈPrinted & Col.ᵈby J.T.Bowen, Philad.ᵃ

Pl. 77.

Audubon's Wood-Warbler?

Strawberry Tree Euonymus Americanus.

1. Male. 2. Female.

Drawn from Nature by J.J.Audubon,F.R.S.F.L.S.

85

Lith⁴Printed & Col⁴by J.T.Bowen,Philad⁴

Pl. 78.

Black-poll'd Wood Warbler.
Black Gum Tree. Nyssa aquatica

1. Males. 2. Female.

86

Drawn from Nature by J.J.Audubon,F.R.S.F.L.S.

Lith^d Printed & Col^d by J. T. Bowen, Philad^a

Pl. 79.

Yellow-throated Wood Warbler.
Chinquapin Castanea pumila.

Male.
87

Drawn from Nature by J.J.Audubon,FRSFLS.   Lith⁴ Printed & Col⁴ by J.T.Bowen. Philad⁴

Pl. 80.

Bay-Breasted Wood-Warbler.

Highland Cotton-plant. Gossipium herbaceum.

1. Male 2. Female

Drawn from Nature by J.J.Audubon,F.R.S.F.L.S.

Lith⁴ Printed & Col⁴ by J. T. Bowen, Philad⁴

Pl. 81.

Chesnut-sided Wood-Warbler.
Moth Mullein. Verbascum Blattaria.

1. Male. 2. Female.

Drawn from Nature by J.J.Audubon,F.R.S.F.L.S.   Lith\d Printed & Col\d by J.T.Bowen, Philad\a

89

Pl. 82.

Pine creeping Wood-Warbler
Yellow Pine Pinus variabilis.
1. Male 2. Female.

Drawn from Nature by J.J.Audubon,FRSFLS.

90

LithPrinted & Colby J.T.Bowen, Philad

Pl. 83.

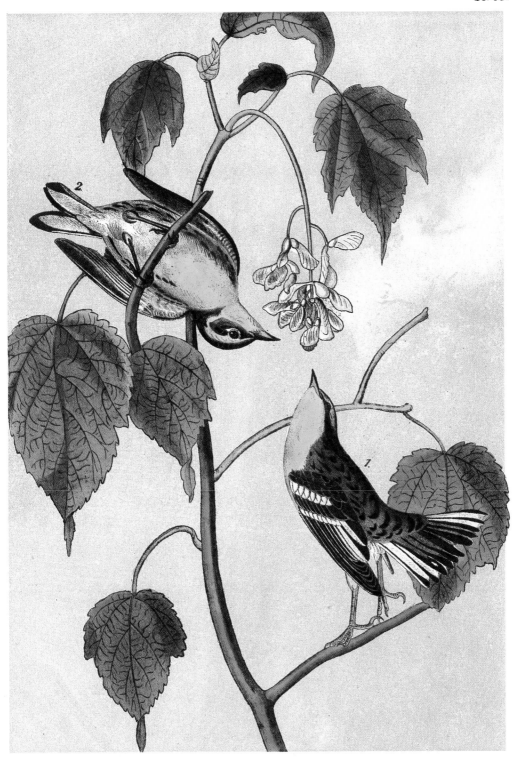

Hemlock Warbler.
Dwarf Maple. Acer Spicatum.

1. Male 2. Female.

Drawn from Nature by J.J.Audubon,F.R.S.F.L.S.

Lith?Printed & Col?by J T Bowen Philad?

Black-throated Green Wood Warbler.
1, Male. 2, Female.
Caprifolium Sempervirens.

Drawn from Nature by J.J.Audubon,F.R.S.F.L.S.

Lith.Printed & Col.by J. T. Bowen, Philad.

Pl. 85

Cape May Wood Warbler.

1. Male 2. Female.

Drawn from Nature by J.J.Audubon,F.R.S.F.L.S.

Lith⁴ Printed & Col⁴ by J. T. Bowen, Philad⁴

Pl. 86.

Caerulean Wood-Warbler.

1. Old Male 2 Young Male.

Bear-berry and Spanish Mulberry.

Drawn from Nature by J.J.Audubon,F.R.S.F.L.S.

94

Lith⁴ Printed & Col⁴ by J. T. Bowen, Philad⁴

Pl. 87.

Blackburnian Wood Warbler.

1. Male 2. Female.

Phlox maculata.

Drawn from Nature by J.J.Audubon, F.R.S.F.L.S.

95

Lith.d Printed & Col.d by J T Bowen, Philad.a

Pl. 88.

Yellow-poll Wood Warbler.

Males.

Drawn from Nature by J.J.Audubon,F.R.S.F.L.S.

96

Lith⁴ Printed & Col⁴ by J. T. Bowen, Philad⁴

Pl. 89

Rathbone's Wood-Warbler.

1. Male 2. Female.

Ramping Trumpet-flower.

Drawn from Nature by J.J.Audubon,F.R.S.F.L.S.

97

Lith.d Printed & Col.d by J.T.Bowen,Philad.a

Pl. 90.

Yellow Red-poll Wood Warbler.

1. Males. 2. Young.

Wild Orange Tree.

Drawn from Nature by J.J.Audubon, F.R.S.F.L.S. 98 Lith^d Printed & Col^d by J.T.Bowen, Philad^a

Pl 91

Blue yellow-backed Wood-Warbler.

1. Male 2. Female.

Louisiana Flag.

Drawn from Nature by J.J.Audubon, F.R.S.F.L.S.   99   Lith⁴ Printed & Col⁴ by J. T. Bowen, Philad⁴

Pl. 92.

R.T.

Townsend's Wood Warbler

Male.

Carolina Allspice.

Drawn from Nature by J.J.Audubon.FRS.FLS   100   Lith⁴ Printed & Col⁴ by J.T.Bowen, Philad⁴.

Pl. 93.

Hermit Wood-Warbler.

1. Male. 2. Female

Strawberry Tree

Drawn from Nature by J.J.Audubon, F.R.S.F.L.S.

101

Lith⁴ Printed & Col⁴ by J. T. Bowen, Philad⁴

Pl. 94.

Black-throated Grey Wood Warbler.

Males.

Drawn from Nature by J.J.Audubon, F.R.S.F.L.S.

102

Lith'd Printed & Col'd by J. T. Bowen, Philad.

Pl. 95

Black-throated Blue Wood-Warbler

1. Male. 2. Female.

Canadian Columbine

Drawn from Nature by J.J.Audubon,F.R.S.FL.S.　　103　　Lith⁴ Printed & Col⁴by J.T.Bowen, Philad⁴

Pl. 96

Black & yellow Wood-Warbler.

1. Male. 2. Female 3. Young.

Flowering Raspberry. Rubus odoratus.

Drawn from Nature by J.J.Audubon,F.R.S.F.L.S.
104
Lith.d Printed & Col.d by J. T. Bowen, Philad.a

Pl. 97

Prairie Wood-Warbler.

1. *Male.* 2. *Female.*

Buffalo Grass.

Drawn from Nature by J.J.Audubon,F.R.S.F.L.S.   105   Lith⁴ Printed & Col⁴ by J.T.Bowen, Philad⁴

Pl. 98.

Blue Mountain Warbler.

Male.

Drawn from Nature by J.J.Audubon,F.R.S.F.L.S.

Lith.ᵈ Printed & Col.ᵈ by J. T. Bowen, Philad.ᵈ

Pl. 99

Connecticut Warbler.

1. Male. 2. Female.

Gentiana Saponaria.

Pl. 100

Macgillivray's Ground Warbler.

1. Male. 2. Female.

Drawn from Nature by J.J.Audubon,F.R.S.F.L.S.

Lith⁴ Printed & Col⁴ by J. T. Bowen, Philad⁴

Pl. 101.

Mourning Ground - Warbler.

Male.

Pheasant's-eye Flos-Adonis.

Drawn from Nature by J.J.Audubon,F.R.S.F.L.S.

109

Lith⁴ Printed & Col⁴ by J. T. Bowen, Phila⁴

Pl. 102.

Maryland Ground-Warbler

1. Adult Male. 2. Young Male. 3. Female.

Wild Olive.

Pl. 103

Delafield's *Ground - Warbler*

Male.

Drawn from Nature by J.J.Audubon.F.R.S.F.L.S.

Lith.d Print.d & Col.d by J T Bowen Philad.ª

111

Pl. 104.

Swainson's Swamp Warbler

Male.

Orange-coloured Azalea. Azalea calendulacea

Drawn from Nature by J.J.Audubon,F.R.S.F.L.S.

Lith.d Printed & Col.d by J.T.Bowen,Philad.a

112

Pl. 105.

Worm-eating Swamp Warbler.

1. Male. 2. Female.

American Poke-weed. Phytolacca decandra.

Drawn from Nature by J.J.Audubon,F.R.S.F.L.S.

Lith.d Printed & Col.d by J. T. Bowen, Philad.a

Pl. 106.

Prothonotary Swamp-Warbler.

1. Male. 2. Female.

Cane Vine.

Drawn from Nature by J.J.Audubon,FRSFLS.

Lith.d Printed & Col.d by J T Bowen Philad.a

114

Pl 107

Golden-winged Swamp-Warbler.

1. Male. 2. Female.

Drawn from Nature by J.J.Audubon.FRS.FLS.   Lith⁴ Printed & Col⁴by J T Bowen Philad⁴

115

Pl. 108.

Bachman's Swamp Warbler.

1. Male. 2. Female.

Gordonia pubescens.

Drawn from Nature by J.J.Audubon.F.R.S.F.L.S.　　　Lith. Printed & Col. by J. T. Bowen, Philad.

Pl. 109.

Carbonated Swamp-Warbler.

Males.

May-bush or Service Pyrus Botryapium.

Drawn from Nature by J.J.Audubon,F.R.S.F.L.S.

Lith.d Printed & Col.d by J. T. Bowen, Philad.a

117

Pl. 110.

Tennessee Swamp Warbler.

Male

Ilex laxifolia.

Drawn from Nature by J.J.Audubon,FRS.FLS. 118 Lith Printed & Col^d by J.T. Bowen Philad

Pl. 111.

Blue-winged Yellow Swamp-Warbler.

1. Male. 2. Female.

Cotton Rose. Hibiscus grandiflorus.

Drawn from Nature by J.J.Audubon,FRSFLS.

119

Lith⁴ Printed & Col⁴ by J. T. Bowen, Philad⁴

Pl. 112.

Orange-crowned Swamp-Warbler.

1. Male. 2. Female.

Huckleberry. Vaccinium frondosum.

Drawn from Nature by J.J.Audubon. S.F.L.S

120

Lith.^d Printed & Col.^d by J. T. Bowen, Philad.^a

Pl. 113.

Nashville Swamp Warbler.

1. Male. 2. Female.

Swamp Spice. Ilex Prinoides

Drawn from Nature by J.J.Audubon F.R.S.F.L.S.

121

Lith⁴ Printed & Col⁴ by J.T.Bowen Philad⁴

Pl. 114.

Black-and-white Creeping Warbler.

Male

Black Larch Pinus-pendula.

Drawn from Nature by J.J.Audubon,FRSFLS.   122   Lith.ᵈPrinted & Col.ᵈby J.T.Bowen,Philad.ᵃ

Pl. 115

Brown Tree-creeper.

1. Male 2. Female.

Pl. 116.

Rock - Wren.

Adult Female.
Smilacina borealis?

Drawn from Nature by J.J.Audubon,F.R.S.F.L.S

Lith⁴ Printed & Col⁴ by J.T.Bowen, Philad⁴

124

Pl. 117.

Great Carolina Wren.

1. Male. 2. Female.

Dwarf Buck-eye. Æsculus. Pavia.

Drawn from Nature by J.J.Audubon, F.R.S.F.L.S.

Lith^d Printed & Col^d by J. T. Bowen, Philad^a

Pl. 118

Bewicks Wren.

Male.

Iron-wood Tree.

Drawn from Nature by J.J.Audubon.FRSFLS.

126

Lith⁴Printed & Col⁴ by J.T.Bowen.Philad⁴

Pl. 119.

Wood Wren.

Male.

Arbutus. Uva - ursi.

Drawn from Nature by J.J.Audubon,F.R.S.F.L.S.

127

Lith.ᵈ Printed & Col.ᵈ by J. T. Bowen, Philad.ᵃ

Pl. 120

House Wren.

1 Male 2 Female 3 Young

In an old Hat

Drawn from Nature by J.J.Audubon,FRSFLS.

Lith\^d Printed & Col\^d by J.T.Bowen, Philad\^a

Pl. 121.

Winter Wren

1. Male 2. Female 3. Young

Drawn from Nature by J.J.Audubon.FRSFLS.   129   Lithd Printed & Cold by J.T.Bowen, Philada

Pl. 122

Parkman's Wren

Male

Pogonia divaricata

Drawn from Nature by J.J.Audubon,F.R.S.F.L.S.

Lith⁴ Printed & Col⁴ by J. T. Bowen, Philad⁴

130

Pl. 123.

Marsh Wren

1. Males. 2 Female & Nest.

Pl. 124.

Short-billed Marsh Wren

1. Male. 2. Female and Nest.

Drawn from Nature by J.J.Audubon,F.R.S.F.L.S.

Lith⁴ Printed & Col⁴ by J.T.Bowen, Philad⁴

Crested Titmouse.

1. Male. 2. Female.

White Pine. Pinus Strobus

Drawn from Nature by J.J.Audubon,F.R.S.F.L.S.   Lith⁴ Printed & Col⁴ by J. T. Bowen, Philad⁴

Pl. 126.

Black cap Titmouse

1. Male. 2. Female.

Plant. Sweet briar.

Drawn from Nature by J.J.Audubon, F.R.S.F.L.S.

Lith.ᵈ Printed & Col.ᵈ by J T Bowen Philadᵃ

Pl. 127.

Carolina Titmouse.

1. Male. 2. Female.

Plant Supple Jack?

Drawn from Nature by J.J.Audubon.F.R.S.F.L.S.

Lith⁴ Printed & Col⁴ by J.T.Bowen, Philad⁴.

Pl. 128

Hudson's Bay Titmouse.

1. Male. 2. Female. 3. Young.

Drawn from Nature by J.J.Audubon,F.R.S.F.L.S.   Lithd Printed & Cold by J. T. Bowen, Philadd.

136

Pl. 129.

Chesnut backed Titmouse.

1. Male. 2. Female.

Drawn from Nature by J.J. Audubon, F.R.S.F.L.S.

Lith⁴ Printed & Col⁴ by J.T. Bowen, Philad⁴

Pl. 130.

Chesnut-crowned Titmouse.

1. *Male.* 2. *Female and Nest.*

Drawn from Nature by J.J.Audubon,F.R.S.F.L.S. 138 Lith⁴ Printed & Col⁴ by J T Bowen, Philad⁴

Pl. 131.

Cuvier's Kinglet.

Male.

Broad-leaved laurel Kalmia latifolia

Drawn from Nature by J.J.Audubon,F.R.S.F.L.S.

139

Lith⁴ Printed & Col⁴ by J. T. Bowen, Philad⁴

Pl. 132

American Golden-crested Kinglet.

1. Male. 2. Female.

Thalia dealbata.

Drawn from Nature by J.J.Audubon.F.R.S.F.L.S.

140

Lith.d Printed & Col.d by J. T Bowen Philad.a

Pl. 133.

Ruby-crowned Kinglet

1. Male. 2. Female.

Kalmia angustifolia.

Drawn from Nature by J.J.Audubon,F.R.S.F.L.S. 141 Lith⁴ Printed & Col⁴ by J. T.Bowen, Philad⁴

Pl 134.

Common Blue Bird?

1. Male. 2. Female. 3. Young.

Great Mullein Verbascum Thapsus

Drawn from Nature by J.J.Audubon,FRS.F.L.S.

Lith⁴ Printed & Col⁴ by J. T. Bowen, Philad⁴.

Pl. 135.

Western Blue Bird?

1. Male. 2. Female.

Drawn from Nature by J.J.Audubon.F.R.S.F.L.S.

Lith. Printed & Col.d by J. T. Bowen, Philad.a

Plate 136

Arctic Blue Bird
Male 1. Female 2

Drawn from Nature by J.J.Audubon,F.R.S.F.L.S   Lith.Printed & Col.d by J.T.Bowen,Phil

Plate 137

American Dipper
Male 1. Female 2.

Drawn from Nature by J.J.Audubon, F.R.S.F.L.S.

Lith. Printed & Col'd by J.T.Bowen, Phil

145

Pl. 138.

Common Mocking Bird

1. Males 1.u. 2. Female 3,

Florida Jessamine, Gelseminum niditum

Rattlesnake.

146

Drawn from Nature by J.J.Audubon, F.R.S.F.L.S.

Lithd Printed & Cold by J. T. Bowen, Philad.

Pl 139

Mountain Mocking Bird

Male

Drawn from Nature by J. J. Audubon, F.R.S. F.L.S.

Lith. Printed & Col.d by J T Bowen, Phil.

Pl. 140.

Cat Bird.

1. Male 2. Female.

Plant Black berry, Rubus villosus.

Drawn from Nature by J.J.Audubon,F.R.S.F.L.S.

Lith⁴ Printed & Col⁴ by J. T. Bowen, Philad⁴

Pl. 141

Ferruginous Mocking Bird?

Males. 1. 2. 3. Female 4.

Drawn from Nature by J.J.Audubon,F.R.S.F.L.S

149

Lith.d Printed & Col.d by J. T Bowen. Philad.

Pl. 142

American Robin, or Migratory Thrush.

1. Male. 2. Female and Young.

Chesnut Oak Quercus prinus.

Drawn from Nature by J.J.Audubon,F.R.S.F.L.S

Lith⁴ Printed & Col⁴by J.T.Bowen, Philad⁴

Pl. 143.

Varied Thrush?

1. Male 2. Female.

American Mistletoe, Viscum verticillatum?

151

Drawn from Nature by J.J.Audubon, F.R.S.F.L.S.

Lith.^d Printed & Col.^d by J. T. Bowen Philad.^a

Pl 144

Wood Thrush.

1. Male. 2. Female.

Common Dogwood.

Drawn from Nature by J.J.Audubon.F.R.S.F.L.S.　　　Lith.Printed & Col.by J.T.Bowen.Philad.

Pl. 145.

Tawny Thrush.

Male;

Habenaria Lacera - Cornus Canadensis

Drawn from Nature by J.J.Audubon,F.R.S.F.L.S.

Lith⁴ Printed & Col⁴ by J. T. Bowen, Philad

Pl. 146.

Hermit Thrush.

1. Male. 2. Female.

Plant Robin Wood.

154

Drawn from Nature by J.J.Audubon, F.R.S.F.L.S.   Lith.d Printed & Col.d by J. T. Bowen, Philad.a

Pl. 147.

Dwarf Thrush.

Male.

Plant Porcelia Triloba.

Drawn from Nature by J.J.Audubon,FRSFLS.

155

Lith⁴Printed & Col⁴ by J.T.Bowen,Philad.

Pl. 148

Golden Crowned Wagtail (Thrush.)

1. Male. 2. Female.

Plant Woody Nightshade.

Drawn from Nature by J.J.Audubon,FRSFLS. 156 Lith.d Printed & Col.d by J. T. Bowen, Philad.a

Pl 149.

Drawn from Nature by J.J.Audubon,F.R.S.F.L.S.

Aquatic. Wood - Wagtail

1. Male. 2. Female.

Plant Indian Turnip

Lith\^d Printed & Col\^d by J. T. Bowen, Philad\^a

Pl. 150.

Drawn from Nature by J.J.Audubon, F.R.S.F.L.S.

American Pipit or Titlark.

1. Male. 2 Female.

Lith^d Printed & Col^d by J. T. Bowen Phil^a.

Pl. 151.

Shore Lark.

1. Male, Summer Plumage. 2. Dº Winter. 3. Female. 4. Young & Nest.

Drawn from Nature by J.J.Audubon, F.R.S.F.L.S.

Lithd. Printed & Cold. by J.T.Bowen, Philad.ª

Pl. 152

Lapland Lark Bunting

1. Male Spring Plumage 2. D.º Winter. 3. Female.

Drawn from Nature by J.J.Audubon,FRSFLS.

Lith.ᵈPrinted & Col.ᵈ by J. T. Bowen, Philad.ᵃ

Pl. 153

Painted Lark - Bunting.

Male.

Drawn from Nature by J.J.Audubon,FR.S.F.L.S.

Lith⁴ Printed & Col⁴ by J.T.Bowen, Philad⁴

Pl. 154

Chesnut-collared Lark Bunting.

Male.

Drawn from Nature by J.J.Audubon,F.R.S.F.L.S.

Lith.⁴Printed & Col.⁴by J.T.Bowen,Philad.ᵃ

Pl. 155.

Black-throated Bunting.

1 Male. 2 Female.

Phalaris arundinacea, and Autirrhinum Linaria.

Drawn from Nature by J.J.Audubon F.R.S.F.L.S.

163

Lith.ᵈ Printed & Col.ᵈ by J.T.Bowen,Philad.ᵃ

Pl. 156.

Snow Lark Bunting.

1. 2 Adult. 3 Young.

Drawn from Nature by J.J.Audubon,F.R.S.F.L.S.

Lith Printed & Col.d by J.T.Bowen Philad.a

Pl. 157.

Townsend's Bunting.

Male.

Drawn from Nature by J.J.Audubon,F.R.S.F.L.S.   Lith⁴Printed & Col⁴by J.T.Bowen,Philad⁴

Pl. 158.

Lark Bunting.

Male.

Drawn from Nature by J.J.Audubon,F.R.S.F.L.S.

166

Lith.ᵈ Printed & Col.ᵈ by J. T. Bowen, Philad.ᵃ

Pl. 159.

Bay-winged Bunting.
Male.
Prickly Pear Cactus Opuntia.

Drawn by J.J. Audubon, F.R.S.F.L.S. Lith. & Cd. by Bowen & Co. Philad^a

Pl. 160.

CLT

Savannah Bunting.

1. Male 2. Female

Indian Pink-root. Spigelia marilandica.

Drawn from Nature by J.J.Audubon F.R.S.FL.S.   Lith^d & Col^d by Bowen & Co Philad^a

Pl. 161.

Clay-coloured Bunting.

Male.

Asclepias tuberosa.

Drawn from Nature by J.J Audubon, F.R.S.F.L.S.

169

Lithd Printed & Cold by J.T.Bowen Philada

Pl. 162.

Yellow-winged Bunting.

Male.

Drawn from Nature by J.J.Audubon,F.R.S.F.L.S.

170

Lith⁴ Printed & Col⁴ by J.T.Bowen Philad⁴

Pl. 163

Shape of tail.

Henslow's Bunting
Male.
Indian Pink-root or Worm-grass
Spigelia Marilandica
Phlox aristata

171

Drawn from Nature by J.J.Audubon.F.R.S.F.L.S. Lith⁴ Printed & Col⁴ by J T Bowen. Philad⁴

Field Bunting.

Male

Calopogon pulchellus. Brown
Dwarf Huckle-berry Vaccinium tenellum

Drawn from Nature by J.J.Audubon.FRSFLS.

172

Lith.d Printed & Col.d by J.T.Bowen Philad.a

Pl. 165

Chipping Bunting.

Male.

"Black locust or False Acacia Robinia pseudacacia."

Drawn from Nature by J.J Audubon, FRS.FLS.

173

Pl 166.

Canada Bunting (Tree Sparrow.)

1. Male 2. Female.

Canadian Barberry.

Drawn from Nature by J.J.Audubon, F.R.S.F.L.S.

174

Lith.d Printed & Col.d by J. T. Bowen, Philad.a

Pl. 167.

Common Snow Bird.

1. Male. 2. Female.

Drawn from Nature by J.J.Audubon,F.R.S.F.L.S.　　　　Lith⁴ Printed & Col⁴ by J.T.Bowen, Philad⁴.

Pl. 168.

Oregon Snow Bird.

1 Male. 2 Female.

Rosa Laevigata?

Drawn from Nature by J.J.Audubon,F.R.S.F.L.S.

176

Lith.ᵈ Printed & Col.ᵈ by J.T.Bowen, Philad.ᵃ

Pl. 169.

Painted Bunting

1. 2. 3. Males in different States of Plumage. 4. Female.

Chicasaw Wild Plum.

Drawn from Nature by J.J.Audubon.F.R.S.F.L.S.

177

Lith⁴ Printed & Col⁴ by J. T. Bowen Philad⁴

Pl. 170.

Indigo Bunting.

1. 2. 3. Males in different States of Plumage. 4. Female.

Wild Sarsaparilla.

Drawn from Nature by J.J.Audubon,F.R.S.F.L.S.　　　　　Lith⁴ Printed & Col⁴ by J. T. Bowen, Philad⁴

Lazuli Finch.

1. Male 2. Female.

Wild Spanish Coffee.

Drawn from Nature by J.J.Audubon,F.R.S.F.L.S.

Lith⁴ Printed & Col⁴ by J. T. Bowen, Philad⁴

Pl. 172.

Sea-side Finch.

1. Male 2. Female.

Carolina Rose.

Drawn from Nature by J.J.Audubon, F.R.S.F.L.S.

Lith! Printed & Col! by J. T. Bowen, Philad.ª

Pl 173.

Macgillivray's Shore-Finch.

1. Male. 2. Female.

Drawn from Nature by J.J.Audubon,F.R.S.F.L.S.

181

Lith⁴ Printed & Col⁴ by J.T.Bowen,Philad⁴

Pl. 174.

Sharp-tailed Finch.

1. Male. 2. Female & Nest.

Drawn from Nature by J.J.Audubon,F.R.S.F.L.S.

Lith.^d Printed & Col.^d by J.T.Bowen, Philad.^a

Pl. 175.

Swamp Sparrow
Male.
May-apple

Drawn from Nature by J.J.Audubon,FRSFLS.

183

Lith⁴ Printed & Col⁴ by J.T.Bowen, Philad⁴

Pl 176.

Bachman's Pinewood Finch.

Male.

Pinckneya pubescens.

Drawn from Nature by J.J.Audubon, F.R.S.F.L.S. Lith.d Printed & Col.d by J. T. Bowen, Philad.a

184

Pl. 177.

Lincoln's Pinewood Finch.

1. Male. 2. Female.

1. Dwarf Cornel 2 Cloudberry 3. Glaucous Kalmia.

Drawn from Nature by J.J.Audubon,FRSFLS.

Lith⁴ Printed & Col⁴ by J.T.Bowen, Philad.

Pl. 178

Mealy Redpoll Linnet.

Male.

Drawn from Nature by J.J.Audubon FRSFLS   Lithd Printed & Cold by J.T.Bowen, Philada

Pl. 179.

Lesser Redpoll Linnet

1. Male. 2. Female.

Drawn from Nature by J.J.Audubon.FRS.FLS.

Lith.d Printed & Col.d by J.T.Bowen.Philad.a

Pl. 180.

Pine Linnet

1 Male 2 Female
Black Larch.

Drawn from Nature by J.J. Audubon. F.R.S.F.L.S.   Lith Printed & Col.d by J.T. Bowen Philad.a

Pl. 181.

American Goldfinch

1. Male. 2. Female.

Common Thistle.

Drawn from Nature by J.J.Audubon,F.R.S.F.L.S

Lith⁴ Printed & Col⁴ by J. T. Bowen, Philad.

Pl. 182.

Black-headed Goldfinch

Male.

Drawn from Nature by J.J.Audubon,F.R.S.F.L.S.　　　　Lith⁴ Printed & Col⁴ by J.T.Bowen,Philad⁴

Pl. 183.

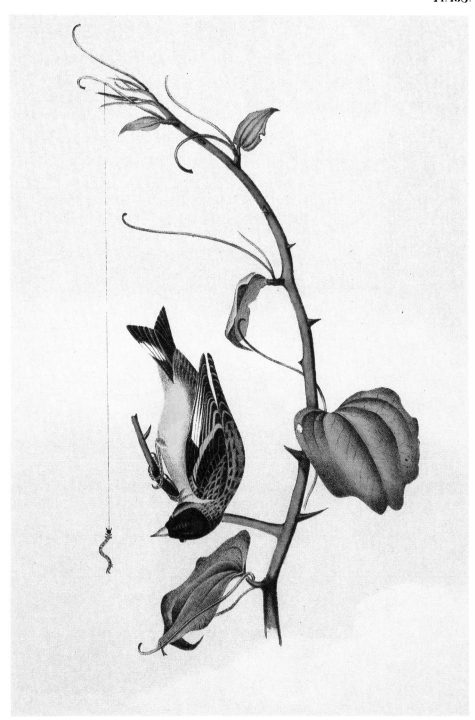

Arkansaw Goldfinch.

Male.

Drawn from Nature by J.J.Audubon. FRSFLS. Lith⁴ Printed & Col⁴ by J. T. Bowen, Philad⁴

Pl. 184.

2.

1.

Yarrell's Goldfinch

1. Male. 2. Female

Drawn from Nature by J.J.Audubon,F.R.S.F.L.S.

Lith^d Printed & Col^d by J.T.Bowen,Philad^a

Pl. 185.

Stanley Goldfinch

Drawn from Nature by J.J.Audubon,F.R.S.F.L.S.

Lith⁴ Printed & Col⁴ by J. T. Bowen, Philad⁴

Pl 186.

Fox-coloured Finch

1. Male. 2. Female.

Drawn from Nature by J.J.Audubon,FRSFLS.

Pl. 187.

Brown Finch

Female.

Drawn from Nature by J.J.Audubon.FRSFLS.

195

Lith.ᵈPrinted & Col.ᵈby J.T.Bowen, Philad.ᵃ

Pl. 188.

Townsend's Finch.

Male.

Drawn from Nature by J.J.Audubon,F.R.S.F.L.S..   Lith.d Printed & Col.d by J. T. Bowen, Philad.a

196

Pl. 189.

Song Finch.

1. Male. 2. Female.

Huckle-berry or Blue tangled Vaccinium frondosum.

Drawn from Nature by J.J.Audubon FRS.FLS 197 Lith⁴ Printed & Col⁴by J.T.Bowen, Philad⁴

Pl. 190

Morton's Finch.

Male.

Drawn from Nature by J.J.Audubon,F.R.S.F.L.S.

Lith. Printed & Col.d by J.T Bowen, Philad.

Pl 191

White-throated Finch.

1. Male. 2. Female.

Common Dogwood.

Drawn from Nature by J.J.Audubon,F.R.S.F.L.S. Lith⁴ Printed & Col⁴ by J.T.Bowen, Philad⁴

Pl. 192.

White-crowned Finch

1. Male. 2. Female.
Wild Summer Grape.

Drawn from Nature by J.J.Audubon.F.R.S.F.L.S.　　　Lith'd Printed & Col'd by J.T.Bowen Philad^a

Pl. 193.

Black-and-yellow-crowned Finch.

Drawn from Nature by J.J.Audubon,F.R.S.F.L.S.

201

Lith.^d Printed & Col.^d by J. T. Bowen, Philad.^a

Pl. 194

Arctic Ground Finch.

1. Male. 2. Female.

Drawn from Nature by J.J.Audubon, F.R.S.F.L.S.

Lith. Printed & Col.d by J. T. Bowen, Philad.a

Pl. 195

Towhe Ground Finch

1. Male. 2. Female.

Common Blackberry

Drawn from Nature by J.J.Audubon,F.R.S.F.L.S.   Lith.ᵈ Printed & Col.ᵈ by J.T.Bowen, Philad.ᵃ

Pl. 196.

Crested Purple Finch
1. Males. 2. Female
Red Larch. Larix Americana.

Drawn from Nature by J.J.Audubon, F.R.S.F.L.S.   Lith⁴ Printed & Col⁴ by J. T. Bowen, Philad⁴

Pl. 197.

Crimson-fronted Purple Finch.
Male.

Drawn from Nature by J.J.Audubon,F.R.S.F.L.S.   Lith⁴ Printed & Col⁴ by J. T. Bowen, Philad⁴

Pl. 198.

Grey-crowned Purple Finch.

Male.

Stokesia cyanea

Drawn from Nature by J.J.Audubon,FRSFLS.

Lith.d Printed & Col.d by J.T.Bowen Philad.a

Pl. 199.

Common Pine-finch

1. Male 2. Female.

Drawn from Nature by J.J.Audubon.FRSFLS.	Lith^{d}Printed & Col^{d}by J.T.Bowen, Philad^a

Common Crossbill.

1. *Males.* 2. *Females.*

Drawn from Nature by J.J.Audubon,F.R.S.F.L.S.

Lith.ᵈ Printed & Col.ᵈ by J. T. Bowen, Philad.ᵃ

Pl. 201.

White-winged Crossbill.

1. Males. 2. Female.

Drawn from Nature by J.J.Audubon,F.R.S.F.L.S.   Lith⁴ Printed & Col⁴ by J.T.Bowen, Philad⁴

Pl. 202.

Prairie Lark Finch.

1 Male. 2 Female.

Drawn from Nature by J.J.Audubon.FRSFLS.

Lith⁴ Printed & Col⁴ by J. T. Bowen, Philad⁴

Pl. 203

Common Cardinal Grosbeak

1. Male. 2. Female

Wild Almond. Prunus caroliniana.

Drawn from Nature by J.J.Audubon,FRSFL.

Lith⁴Printed & Col⁴by J.T.Bowen,Philad⁴

Pl. 204.

Blue Song Grosbeak

1. Male 2. Female 3 Young.

Drawn from Nature by J.J.Audubon,F.R.S.F.L.S.   Lith⁴ Printed & Col⁴ by J.T.Bowen, Philad⁴

212

Pl. 205.

Rose-breasted Song-Grosbeak
1. Males. 2. Female. 3. Young Male.
Ground Hemlock Taxus canadensis.

Drawn from Nature by J.J.Audubon,F.R.S.F.L.S. Lith⁴ Printed & Col⁴by J.T.Bowen, Philad⁴

Pl. 206

Black-headed Song-Grosbeak.

1. Male. 2. Female.

Drawn from Nature by J.J.Audubon,F.R.S.F.L.S.

Lith⁴ Printed & Col⁴by J. T. Bowen, Philad⁴

Pl. 207.

Evening Grosbeak.

1. Male. 2. Female 3. Young Male.

Drawn from Nature by J.J.Audubon,F.R.S.F.L.S.

Lith⁴ Printed & Col⁴ by J. T. Bowen, Philad⁴

Pl. 208.

Summer Red-bird

1. Male. 2. Female 3. Young Male.

Wild Muscadine. Vitis rotundifolia. Mich

Drawn from Nature by J.J.Audubon,F.R.S.F.L.S.   Lith.ᵈPrinted & Col.ᵈby J.T.Bowen,Philad.ᵃ

Pl. 209.

Scarlet Tanager

1. Male. 2. Female.

Drawn from Nature by J.J.Audubon, F.R.S.F.L.S.

217

Lith.d Printed & Col.d by J. T. Bowen, Philad.a

Pl 210.

Louisiana Tanager.

1. Males. 2. Female.

Drawn from Nature by J.J.Audubon,F.R.S.F.L.S.　　　　Lith⁴ Printed & Col⁴ by J.T.Bowen, Philad⁴

218

Pl. 211

Wandering Rice-bird.
1. Male. 2. Female.
Red Maple Acer Rubrum.

Drawn from Nature by J.J.Audubon.F.R.S.F.L.S.   Lith^d Printed & Col^d by J. T. Bowen, Philad^a

Pl 212.

Common Cow-bird.

1. Male. 2. Female. 3. Young.

Drawn from Nature by J.J.Audubon.FRSFLS.

Lith^d Printed & Col^d by J T Bowen. Phil^{ad}

Pl. 213

Saffron-headed Marsh-Blackbird

1. Male. 2. Female 3. Young Male.

Drawn from Nature by J.J.Audubon.FRSFLS.   Lith⁴ Printed & Col⁴ by J T Bowen, Phila⁴.

Pl. 214.

Red-and-white-shouldered Marsh Blackbird.
Male.

Drawn from Nature by J.J.Audubon,FRS,FLS.   Lith⁴ Printed & Col⁴ by J. T. Bowen, Philad⁴

Pl 215

Red-and-black-shouldered Marsh-Blackbird.

1. Male 2. Female.

Drawn from Nature by J.J.Audubon,F.R.S.F.L.S.   Lith⁴Printed & Col⁴by J.T.Bowen,Philad⁵

Pl 216.

Red-winged Starling

1. Male Adult 2. Young Male 3. Female

Red Maple.

Drawn from Nature by J.J Audubon FRSFLS

Lith⁴ Printed & Col⁴ by J. T. Bowen, Philad⁴

Pl. 217

Baltimore Oriole, or Hang-nest.

1. Male. Adult. 2. Young Male. 3. Female.

Tulip Tree.

Drawn from Nature by J.J.Audubon.F.R.S.F.L.S.   Lith⁴ Printed & Col⁴ by J.T.Bowen, Philad⁴

Bullock's Troopial.

1. Male Adult. 2 Young Male 3. Female
Caprifolium flavum.

Drawn from Nature by J.J. Audubon, F.R.S.F.L.S.   Lith? Printed & Col? by J. T. Bowen, Philad?

Pl. 219.

Orchard Oriole, or Hang nest.
1. Male adult. 2. Young Male. 3. Female & Nest.
Honey Locust.

Drawn from Nature by J.J.Audubon, F.R.S.F.L.S.   Lith.d Printed & Col.d by J.T.Bowen Philad.a

Pl. 220.

Boat-tailed Grackle.

1. Male. 2. Female.

Live Oak.

Drawn from Nature by J.J.Audubon.F.R.S.F.L.S.

lith⁴ Printed & Col⁴ by J.T.Bowen. Philad⁴

Common, or Purple Crow Blackbird.

1 Male 2 Female

Maize or Indian Corn.

Drawn from Nature by J.J.Audubon,F.R.S.F.L.S

Lith⁴ Printed & Col⁴ by J.T Bowen, Philad⁴

229

Pl. 222.

Rusty Crow Blackbird.
1. Male. 2. Female. 3. Young.
Black Haw.

Drawn from Nature by J.J.Audubon,FRSFLS.   Lith.ᵈPrinted & Col.ᵈby J.T.Bowen,Philad.ᵃ

Pl. 223

Meadow Starling or Meadow Lark
1. Males. 2. Female and Nest.
Yellow flowered Gerardia.

Drawn from Nature by J.J.Audubon, F.R.S.F.L.S.

Lith.d Printed & Col.d by J. T. Bowen, Philad.a

Pl 224

Raven.

Old Male

Thick Shell bark Hickory.

Drawn from Nature by J.J.Audubon,F.R.S.F.L.S.

Lith⁴ Printed & Col⁴ by J.T.Bowen, Philad⁴

232

Pl. 225.

Common American Crow.

Male.

Black Walnut.

Drawn from Nature by J.J.Audubon.FRS.FLS.   Lith.ᵈPrinted & Col.ᵈby J. T. Bowen, Philad.ᵃ

Pl 226.

Fish Crow.

1. Male. 2. Female.
Honey Locust.

Drawn from Nature by J.J.Audubon,F.R.S.F.L.S.

Lith⁴ Printed & Col⁴ by J. T. Bowen, Philad⁴

234

Pl. 227.

Common Magpie

1 Male 2 Female

Drawn from Nature by J.J.Audubon,F.R.S.F.L.S.   Lith⁴Printed & Col⁴by J.T.Bowen Philad⁴

Pl. 228.

Yellow billed Magpie
Male.
Plantanus

Drawn from Nature by J.J.Audubon.FRSFLS   Lith.d Printed & Col.d by J T Bowen Philad.a

Pl 229.

Columbia Magpie or Jay.

Males.

Drawn from Nature by J.J.Audubon.FRS.FLS.

Lith.d Printed & Col.d by J.T.Bowen Philad.a

Pl. 230

Stellers Jay.

Male.

Drawn from Nature by J.J.Audubon,FRSFLS.

Lith⁴ Printed & Col⁴ by J. T. Bowen, Philad⁴

238

Pl. 231.

Blue Jay

1. Male. 2 & 3 Female.

Trumpet-flower. Bignonia radicans.

Drawn from Nature by J.J.Audubon,F.R.S.F.L.S

Lith⁴Printed & Col⁴by J.T.Bowen, Philad⁴

Pl. 232.

Ultramarine Jay.

Adult Male.

Drawn from Nature by J.J.Audubon.F.R.S.F.L.S.

Lith.ᵈPrinted & Col.ᵈby J.T.Bowen, Philad.ᵈ

Pl. 233.

Florida Jay.
1. Male. 2. Female.
Persimon tree Diospyros Virginiana.

Drawn from Nature by J.J.Audubon,FRSFLS.

Lith Printed & Col^d by J.T.Bowen Phila^d

Canada Jay.

1. Male. 2. Female. 3 Young.

White Oak. Quercus alba.

Drawn from Nature by J.J.Audubon.FRS.FLS.   Lith.d Printed & Col.d by J T.Bowen Philad.a

Pl. 235.

Clarke's Nutcracker.

1. Male. 2. Female.

Drawn from Nature by J.J.Audubon,F.R.S.F.L.S.

Lith⁴ Printed & Col⁴ by J. T. Bowen, Philad⁴

Pl 236.

Great American Shrike.

1. Male 2. Female 3. Young.

Crataegus Apiifolia

Drawn from Nature by J.J.Audubon,F.R.S.F.L.S.   Lithd Printed & Cold by J. T. Bowen, Philada

Pl. 237.

Loggerhead Shrike.

1. Male 2. Female.

Greenbriar or Round-leaved Smilax Smilax Rotundifolia.

Drawn from Nature by J.J.Audubon,F.R.S.F.L.S.

Lith.ᵈPrinted & Col.ᵈby J.T.Bowen,Philad.ᵃ

Pl. 238.

Yellow-throated Vireo, or Greenlet.
Male
Swamp Snowball. Hydrangea quercifolia.

Drawn from Nature by J.J.Audubon.FRSFLS

Lith.d Printed & Col.d by J. T. Bowen Philad.a

Pl 239

Solitary Vireo or Greenlet

1. Male. 2. Female.

American Cane . Miegia macrosperma.

Drawn from Nature by J.J.Audubon F.R.S.F.L.S.   Lith⁴ Printed & Col⁴ by J.T.Bowen Phil⁴

Pl. 240.

White-eyed Vireo or Greenlet.
Male.
Pride of China, or bead tree. Melia Azedarach.

Drawn from Nature by J.J.Audubon,F.R.S.F.L.S.   Lith⁴Printed & Col⁴by J.T.Bowen,Phila⁴

248

Pl. 241.

Warbling Vireo or Greenlet.

1. Male. 2. Female.

Swamp Magnolia.

Drawn from Nature by J.J.Audubon, FRS.FLS.

Lith⁴ Printed & Col⁴ by J T Bowen Philad⁴.

Pl. 242

Bartrams Vireo or Greenlet.

Male.
Ipomœa.

Drawn from Nature by J.J.Audubon,F.R.S.F.L.S.   250   Lith⁴ Printed & Col⁴ by J.T Bowen, Philad⁴

Pl. 243

Red-eyed Vireo or Greenlet

Male

Honey locust

Drawn from Nature by J.J.Audubon.FRSFLS

251

Lith.d Printed & Cold by J.T.Bowen Philad.a

Pl. 244

Yellow breasted Chat

1 2 3 Male 4 Female

Green briar

Pl 245.

Black throated Wax-wing.
or Bohemian Chatterer.

1. Male. 2. Female

Canadian Service Tree

Drawn from Nature by J.J.Audubon,F.R.S.F.L.S.   Lith.ᵈPrinted & Col.ᵈby J. T. Bowen, Philad.ᵃ

Pl. 246.

Cedar bird, or Cedar Wax-wing.

1 Male 2 Female.

Red Cedar.

Drawn from Nature by J.J. Audubon FRS FLS.   Lith⁴ Printed & Col⁴ by J. T. Bowen, Philad⁴

Pl. 247.

White-breasted Nuthatch.

1. Male. 2. & 3. Female.

Drawn from Nature by J.J.Audubon,F.R.S.F.L.S.

Lith⁴ Printed & Col⁴ by J. T. Bowen, Philad⁴

Pl. 248.

Red-billed Nuthatch.

1 Male. 2 Female.

Drawn from Nature by J.J.Audubon,F.R.S.F.L.S

Lith.d Printed & Col.d by J.T.Bowen, Philad.a

256

Pl. 249.

Brown headed Nuthatch.

1 Male. 2. Female.

Drawn from Nature by J.J.Audubon.FRSFLS

Lith⁴ Printed & Col⁴ by J.T.Bowen Philad⁴

Pl. 260.

Californian Nuthatch.

Adults.

Drawn from Nature by J.J.Audubon,FRSFLS   Lith Printed & Col^d by J.T.Bowen, Phila^d

Pl. 251.

Mango Humming bird.

1. 2. *Males.* 3. *Female.*

Bignonia grandifolia.

Drawn from Nature by J.J.Audubon,F.R.S.F.L.S.

Lith⁴ Printed & Col⁴ by J. T Bowen, Philad⁴

Pl. 252.

Anna Humming bird.

1. 2. Males. 3 Female.

Hibiscus Virginicus.

Drawn from Nature by J.J.Audubon,FRSFLS.　　　　　Lith⁴Printed & Col⁴by J.T. Bowen. Philad⁴

Pl. 253

Ruby-throated Humming bird

1. 2. Males. 3 Female. 4. Young.

Bignonia radicans.

Drawn from Nature by J.J.Audubon,FRSFLS

Lith⁴ Printed & Col⁴ by J.T.Bowen, Philad⁴

Pl 254

Ruff-necked Humming bird.
1. 2. Males 3 Female.
Cleome heptaphylla.

Drawn from Nature by J.J.Audubon.FRS.FLS.   Lith⁴ Printed & Col⁴ by J. T. Bowen. Philad⁴

Pl. 255.

Belted Kingfisher.
Alcedo Alcyon.
1. Males. 2. Female

Drawn from Nature by J.J.Audubon, F.R.S.F.L.S.

Lith & Col.d by Bowen & Co. Philad.a

263

Pl 256

Ivory-billed Woodpecker.

1. Male. 2. Female.

Drawn from Nature by J.J.Audubon, FRSFLS.

Lith⁴ Printed & Col⁴ by J T Bowen Philad⁴

Pileated Woodpecker.

1. Adult Male. 2. Adult Female 3 and 4. Young Males

Raccoon Grape.

Drawn from Nature by J.J.Audubon.F.R.S.F.L.S.

Lith⁴Printed & Col⁴by J. T. Bowen, Philad⁴

Pl. 258.

Canadian Woodpecker.

Male.

Drawn from Nature by J.J.Audubon,F.R.S.F.L.S.

Lith.d Printed & Col.d by J. T. Bowen, Philad.a

Pl. 259.

Phillips Woodpecker.

Males.

Drawn from Nature by J.J.Audubon.FRS.FLS   Lith.d Printed & Col.d by J.T.Bowen Philad.a

Pl. 260.

Maria's Woodpecker.

1. Male. 2. Female.

Drawn from Nature by J.J.Audubon, F.R.S.F.L.S.   Lith.ᵈ Printed & Col.ᵈ by J.T.Bowen, Philad.ᵃ

Pl 261

Harris's Woodpecker.

1. *Male.* 2. *Female.*

Drawn from Nature by J.J.Audubon F.R.S.F.L.S.   Lith.ᵈPrinted & Col.ᵈby J. T. Bowen, Philad.ᵃ

Pl. 262.

Hairy Woodpecker.

1. Male. 2. Female.

Drawn from Nature by J.J.Audubon,FRSFLS.

Lith⁴ Printed & Col⁴ by J. T. Bowen, Philad⁴

Pl. 263.

Downy Woodpecker.

1. Male. 2. Female.

Drawn from Nature by J.J.Audubon,FRSFLS.

Lithd Printed & Cold by J T Bowen Philada

Pl. 264.

Red-cockaded Woodpecker.

1. 2. Males 3. Female.

Pl. 265.

Audubons Woodpecker.

Male.

Drawn from Nature by J.J.Audubon,FRSFLS.

Lith⁴ Printed & Col⁴ by J.T.Bowen, Philad⁴

Pl. 266.

Red-breasted Woodpecker.

1. Male. 2. Female.

Drawn from Nature by J.J.Audubon,F.R.S.F.L.S.

Lith⁴ Printed & Col⁴ by J.T.Bowen, Philad⁸

Pl. 267.

Yellow-bellied Woodpecker.

1. Male. 2. Female.

Prunus Caroliniana.

Drawn from Nature by J.J.Audubon.F.R.S.F.L.S

275

Lithᵈ Printed & Colᵈ by J.T. Bowen, Philadᵃ

Pl. 268

Arctic three-toed Woodpecker.

1. 2. Males. 3. Female.

Drawn from Nature by J.J.Audubon,FRSFLS.

276

Lith⁴ Printed & Col⁴ by J.T.Bowen,Philad⁴

Pl. 269.

Banded three-toed Woodpecker

1. Male 2. Female.

Drawn from Nature by J.J.Audubon,F.R.S.F.L.S   - Lith⁴ Printed & Col⁴ by J T Bowen, Philad⁴

Pl. 270.

Red-bellied Woodpecker.

1. Male. 2. Female.

Drawn from Nature by J.J.Audubon,F.R.S.F.L.S.

Lith.d Printed & Col.d by J.T.Bowen, Philad.a

Pl. 271

Red-headed Woodpecker

1. Male. 2. Female. 3. Young.

Drawn from Nature by J.J.Audubon,F.R.S.F.L.S.

Lith^d Printed & Col^d by J. T. Bowen, Philad^a

Pl 272

Lewis' Woodpecker.

1. Male 2. Female.

Drawn from Nature by J.J.Audubon,F.R.S.F.L.S.   Lith.d Printed & Col.d by J. T. Bowen, Phila.

Pl 273

Golden-winged Woodpecker.

1. Male 2. Females.

Drawn from Nature by J.J.Audubon, F.R.S.F.L.S.   Lith^d Printed & Col^d by J.T.Bowen, Philad^a

281

Pl. 274

Red-shafted Woodpecker.

1. Male. 2. Female.

Drawn from Nature by J.J.Audubon,F.R.S.F.L.S.

Lith⁴ Printed & Col⁴ by J. T. Bowen, Philad⁴

Pl. 275.

Yellow-billed Cuckoo
1 Male. 2 Female.
Papaw Tree

Drawn from Nature by J.J.Audubon,F.R.S.F.L.S.

Lith.Printed & Col.d by J.T.Bowen Philad.

283

Pl 276

Black-billed Cuckoo.

1. Male 2. Female

Magnolia grandiflora

Drawn from Nature by J.J. Audubon, F.R.S.F.L.S.

284

Pl. 277.

Mangrove Cuckoo.
Male.
Seven years apple.

Drawn from Nature by J.J.Audubon.FRS.FLS.

Lith⁴Printed & Col⁴by J. T. Bowen, Philad⁴

Pl.278.

Carolina Parrot or Parrakeet

1.2. Males 3. Female. 4. Young.

Cockle bur.

Drawn from Nature by J.J.Audubon,F.R.S.F.L.S.

Lith⁴ Printed & Col⁴ by J. T. Bowen, Philad⁴

Pl. 279

Band-tailed Dove or Pigeon?

1. Male 2. Female.
Cornus Nuttalli!!

Drawn from Nature by J.J.Audubon.FRS.FLS.

Lith⁴ Printed & Col⁴ by J.T Bowen, Philad⁴

Pl 280

White headed Dove, or Pigeon.

1. Male 2. Female.

Cordia sebestina.

Drawn from nature by J.W. Audubon.

Lith & col. by Bowen & Co. Philad.ᵃ

Pl. 281.

Zenaida Dove.

1. Male 2. Female
Anona.

Drawn from Nature by J.J.Audubon,F.R.S.F.L.s.   Lith⁴Printed & Col⁴by J T Bowen, Philad⁴

Pl. 282.

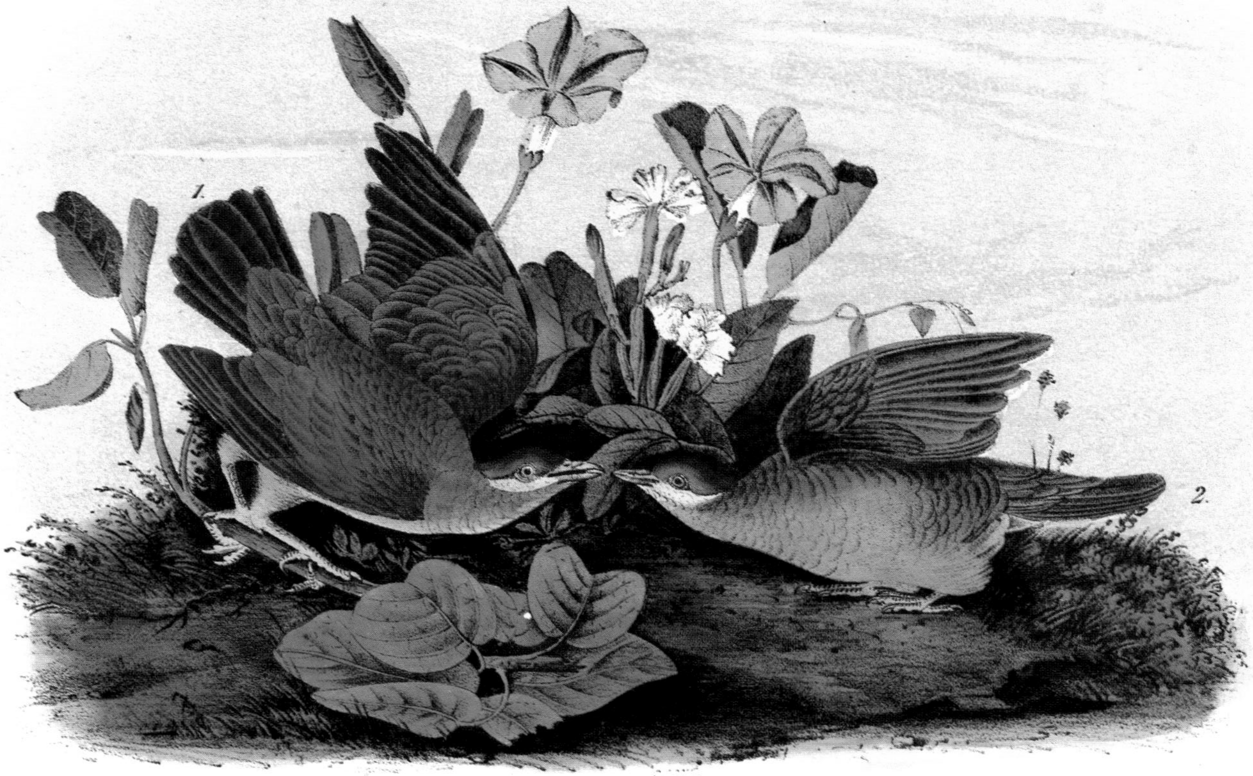

Key-West Dove.

1. Male. 2. Female.

Pl. 283

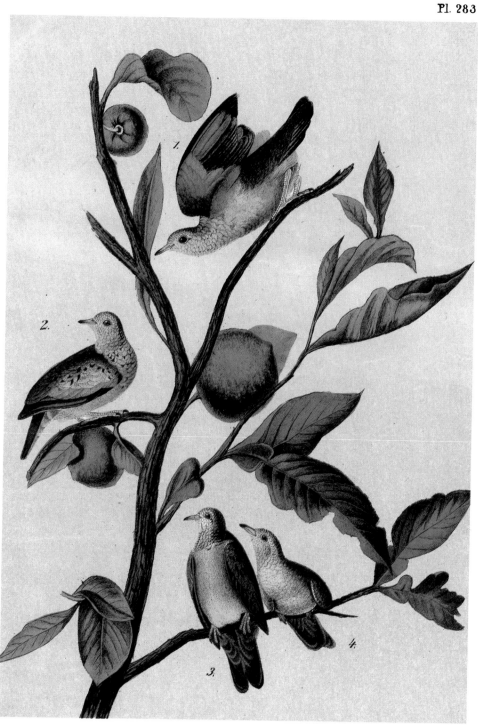

Ground Dove.

1. & 2. Males. 3. Female. 4. Young.

Drawn from Nature by J.J.Audubon.F.R.S.F.L.S.   *Wild Orange.*   Lith⁴ᵈPrinted & Col⁴ᵈby J.T.Bowen, Philad⁴ᵃ

Pl. 284.

Blue headed Ground Dove or Pigeon.

1. Male. 2. Females.

Drawn from Nature by J.J.Audubon.F.R.S.F.L.S.

Lith.d Printed & Col.d by J. T. Bowen, Phila.d

Pl. 285.

Passenger Pigeon.

1. Male. 2. Female.

Drawn from Nature by J. J. Audubon, F.R.S.F.L.S.　　　　　Lith. & col. Bowen & Co. Philada.

Pl. 286.

Carolina Turtle Dove.

1. Males. 2. Females.

Drawn from Nature by J.J.Audubon,F.R.S.F.L.S.

Lith & col. Bowen & Co. Philada.

Pl. 287.

On Stone by Max Rosenthal.

Wild Turkey.
Male.

Drawn from Nature by J.J.Audubon,F.R.S.FL.S.   Lith. & col. Bowen & Co. Philada.

PL.288.

Drawn from Nature by J.J.Audubon,F.R.S.F.L.S.

Max Rosenthal del

Wild Turkey. Female & Young.

Bowen & Co. lith &col.Philada.

296

Pl. 289

Common American Partridge.

1. Male. 2. Female. 3. Young.

Drawn from Nature by J.J.Audubon,F.R.S.F.L.S.

Lith.d Printed & Col.d by J. T. Bowen, Phil.d

Pl. 290.

California Partridge.

1. Male. 2. Female.

Drawn from Nature by J.J.Audubon.FRSFLS.

Lith Printed & Col.d by J T Bowen Philad.a

Pl. 291.

Plumed Partridge.

1. Male 2. Female

Drawn from Nature by J.J.Audubon,FRS.FLS.

Lith.d Printed & Col.d by J. T. Bowen, Philad.a

Pl. 292.

Welcome Partridge.

Young

Pl. 293.

Ruffed Grouse.
1. 2. Males. 3. Female.

Drawn from Nature by J.J.Audubon.FRSFLS

Lith.d Printed & Col.d by J T Bowen. Phila.d

PL. 294.

Canada Grouse?
1, 2. Males 3 Females.
4. Trillium pictum 5. Streptopus distortus.

Pl. 295.

Drawn from Nature by J.J.Audubon, F.R.S.F.L.S.

Dusky Grouse.
1. Male. 2. Female.

LithPrinted & Col^d by J.T.Bowen, Philad^a

303

Pl. 296.

Drawn from Nature by J.J.Audubon,FRS.FLS.

Lith^d.Printed & Col^d by J.T.Bowen, Philad^a.

Pinnated Grouse.

1.2. Males. 3 Female. Lilium Superbum.

Pl. 297.

Drawn from Nature by J.J.Audubon, F.R.S.F.L.S.

Cock of the Plains.

1. Male. 2. Female.

Lith.d Printed & Col.d by J. T. Bowen, Philad.a

305

Pl 298.

Sharp-tailed Grouse.

1. Male 2. Female.

Drawn from Nature by J.J.Audubon.F.R.S.F.L.S.

Lith.Printed.& Col.d by J.T.Bowen Philad.a

Pl. 299.

Willow Ptarmigan
1. Male. 2. Female & Young.

Drawn from Nature by J.J.Audubon,F.R.S.F.L.S.

Lith^d.Printed & Col^d.by J.T.Bowen. Philad.^a

Pl. 300

American Ptarmigan?

Male.

Drawn from Nature by J.J.Audubon,FRS.F.L.S.

Lith^d Printed & Col^d by J.T.Bowen, Philad^a

Pl. 301

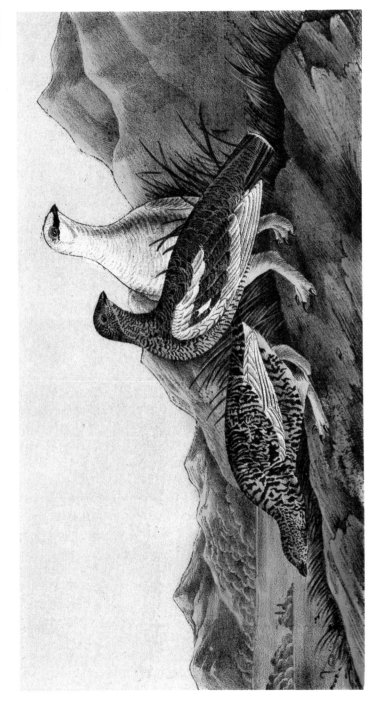

Rock Ptarmigan.

1. Male, in Winter. 2. Female, Summer Plumage. 3. Young in August.

Drawn from Nature by J.J.Audubon.FRS.FLS.

Lith.d Printed & Col.d by J.T.Bowen, Philad.a

Pl. 302

White-tailed Ptarmigan.

Adult, in Winter Plumage.

Drawn from Nature by J.J.Audubon.F.R.S.F.L.S.

Lith.d Printed & Col.d by J.T.Bowen. Philad.a

Pl. 303.

Drawn from Nature by J.J.Audubon,F.R.S.F.L.S.

Purple Gallinule

Adult Male. Spring Plumage.

Lith.Printed & Col.d by J.T.Bowen Philad.a

Pl. 304.

Drawn from Nature by J.J.Audubon.FRS.FLS.

Common Gallinule.

Adult Male.

Lith. Printed & Col.d by J.T.Bowen Philad.

Pl. 305

Drawn from Nature by I.J.Audubon,FRSFLS

American Coot

Lith¹ Printed & Col⁴ by J T Bowen.

Pl 306.

Sora Rail.

1. Male. 2. Female. 3. Young.

Drawn from Nature by J.J.Audubon.F.R.S.F.L.S

Lith.d Printed & Col.d by J. T. Bowen Philad.a

Pl. 307.

Yellow-breasted Rail.

Adult Male in Spring.

Drawn from Nature by J.J.Audubon. F.R.S.F.L.S.

Lith.ᵈPrinted & Col.ᵈ by J T Bowen, Philad.ᵃ

Pl. 308.

Least Water=Rail.

1. Adult Male. 2. Young.

Drawn from Nature by J.J.Audubon.F.R.S.F.L.S.

Lith.d Printed & Col.d by J.T.Bowen Philad.a

316

Pl. 309.

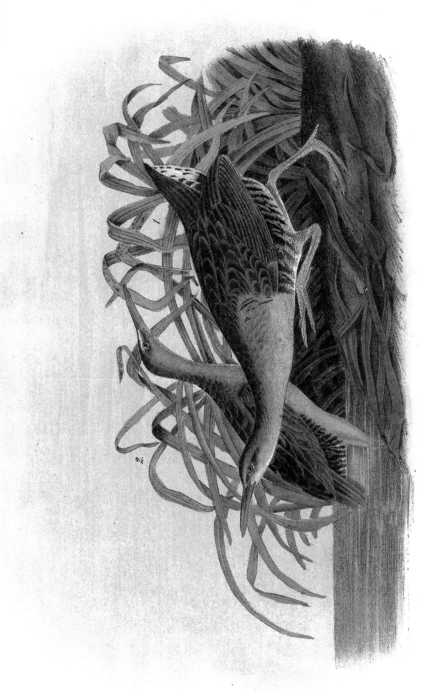

Drawn from Nature by J.J.Audubon.FRS.FLS.

Great Red-breasted Rail, or fresh-water, Marsh Hen.

1. Male adult. 2. Young.

Lith.d Printed & Col.d by J.T.Bowen, Philad.a

Pl. 310.

Clapper Rail or Salt Water Marsh Hen.

1. Male. 2. Female.

Drawn from Nature by J.J.Audubon,F.R.S.F.L.S.

Lith⁴.Printed & Col⁴.by J.T.Bowen,Philad⁴.

318

Pl. 311.

Virginian Rail.

1. Male. 2. Female. 3. Young.

Drawn from Nature by J.J. Audubon, F.R.S.F.L.S.

Lith Printed & Col'd by J T Bowen, Philad"

Pl. 312.

Scolopaceus Courlan.

Drawn from Nature by J.J.Audubon,F.R.S.F.L.S.

Lith.d Printed & Col.d by J. T. Bowen, Philad.a

Pl. 313.

Whooping Crane.

Male, adult.

Drawn from Nature by J.J.Audubon, F.R.S.E.L.S.   Lith⁴ Printed & Col⁴ by J. T. Bowen, Philad⁴

Pl. 314.

Whooping Crane.

Drawn from Nature by J.J.Audubon, F.R.S.F.L.S.   *Young.*   Lith.ᵈ Printed & Col.ᵈ by J.T.Bowen, Philad.ᵃ

Pl. 315.

Black-bellied Plover

1. Male. 2. Young in Autumn 3. Nestling.

Drawn from Nature by J.J.Audubon,FRSFLS.

Lith.d Printed & Col.d by J T Bowen, Philad.a

Pl 316.

American Golden Plover.

1 Summer Plumage. 2 Winter. 3 Variety in March.

324

Pl. 317.

Kildeer Plover ?

1 Male 2. Female.

Drawn from Nature by J.J.Audubon.FRSFLS

Lith.ᵈPrinted & Colᵈby J.T.Bowen Phil.ᵈ

Pl. 318.

Drawn from Nature by J.J.Audubon,F.R.S.F.L.S.

Rocky Mountain Plover

Female.

Lith.d Printed & Col.d by J.T Bowen Philad.a

Wilson's Plover.

1. Male. 2. Female.

Drawn from Nature by J.J Audubon.F.R.S.F.L.S.

Lith Printed & Col^d by J T Bowen, Philad^a

327

Pl. 320.

American Ring Plover

Drawn from Nature by J.J.Audubon.FRSFLS.

1. Adult. Male. 2. Young in August.

Lith.d Printed & Col.d by J T Bowen Philad.a

Pl. 331

Piping Plover
1 Male 2 Female

PL. 322

Townsend's Surf Bird

Females

Drawn from Nature by J.J. Audubon FRS FLS

Lith Printed & Col'd by J.T. Bowen Phil.ad.a

330

Pl. 323

Turnstone.
1 Summer Plumage 2 Winter

Drawn from Nature by J.J.Audubon, FRSFLS

Lith^d Printed & Col^d by J T Bowen, Philad^a

Pl. 321

R.T.

American Oyster Catcher

Male

Drawn from Nature by J.J Audubon.F.R.S.F.L.S.

Lith.d Printed & Col.d by J T Bowen Philad.a

Pl. 325

Bachman's Oyster-catcher.

Male

Pl. 326.

Drawn from Nature by J.J. Audubon F.R.S.F.L.S.

Lith.d Printed & Col.d By J. T. Bowen. Philad.a

Townsend's Oyster-catcher.

Female.

Pl. 327.

Drawn from Nature by J.J.Audubon,FRS.FLS.

Bartramian Sandpiper

1. Male. 2. Female.

Lith. Printed & Col⁴ by J. T. Bowen, Philad.

335

Pl. 328.

Red-breasted Sandpiper

1. Summer Plumage 2. Winter.

Drawn from Nature by J.J.Audubon,FRSFLS.

Lith.d Printed & Col.d by J T Bowen, Philad.a

Pl. 329.

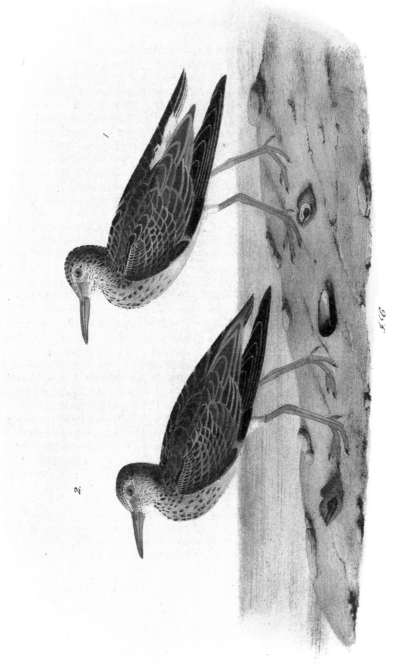

Drawn from Nature by J.J. Audubon, F.R.S.F.L.S.

Lith.d Printed & Col.d by J T Bowen, Philad.a

Pectoral Sandpiper.

1. Male 2. Female.

Pl. 330.

Purple Sandpiper.

1. Summer. 2. Winter.

338

Pl 331

Buff breasted Sand-piper
1 Male 2 Female.

Drawn from Nature by J.J Audubon FRSFLS.

Lith⁴ Printed & Col⁴ by J T Bowen, Philad⁴

Pl. 332.

Red-backed Sandpiper.
1. Summer Plumage. 2. Winter.

Pl. 333.

Curlew Sandpiper

1. Adult Male. 2. Young.

Drawn from Nature by J.J. Audubon, FRSFLS

Lith. Printed & Col.d by J.T. Bowen, Philad.a

Pl. 334.

Drawn from Nature by J.J.Audubon.FRS.FLS

Long-legged Sandpiper.

Lith.Printed & Col.d by J T Bowen Philad.

Pl. 335

Schinz's Sandpiper

1. Male 2. Female.

Drawn from Nature by J.J Audubon, FRSFLS.

Lith Printed & Col.d by. J. T. Bowen, Phil.ad.

Pl. 336.

Semipalmated Sandpiper.

1. Summer Plumage. 2. Winter.

Drawn from Nature by J.J. Audubon, F.R.S.F.L.s.

Lith. Printed & Col. by J.T. Bowen Philad.

Pl. 337

Little Sandpiper.

1. Male Summer Plumage. 2. Female.

Drawn from Nature by J.J Audubon, F.R.S.F.L.S.

Lith Printed & Col by J T Bowen, Philad.

Pl. 338.

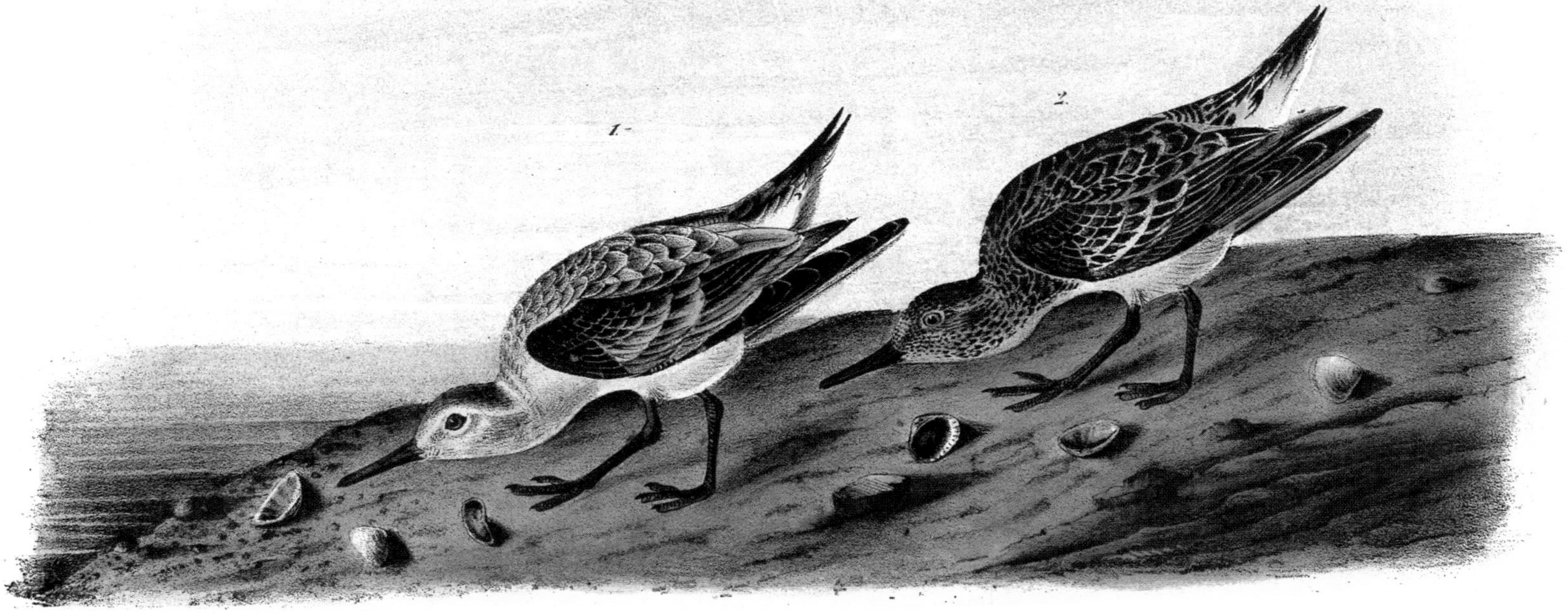

Sanderling Sandpiper
1. Winter plumage. 2. Summer.

Pl. 339.

Red Phalarope

1. Adult Male. 2. Winter plumage.

Drawn from Nature by J.J.Audubon F.R.S.F.L.S.

Lith.d Printed & Col.d by J T Bowen Philad.a

Pl. 340

Hyperborean Phalarope!

1. Male. 2. Female. 3. Young in autumn.

Drawn from Nature by J.J.Audubon.F.R.S.F.L.S.

Lith.Printed & Col.d by J.T.Bowen, Philad.a

Pl.341.

Wilsons Phalarope
1. Male. 2. Female.

Drawn from Nature by J. J. Audubon, F.R.S. F.L.S.

Lith. Printed & col.d by J. T. Bowen, Phila.

Pl. 342.

Spotted Sandpiper

1. Male. 2. Female.

Drawn from Nature by J.J. Audubon, F.R.S.F.L.S.

Lith. Printed & Col.d by J T Bowen Philad.a

Pl. 343.

Drawn from Nature by J.J.Audubon, F.R.S.F.L.S.

Solitary Sandpiper.

1. Male. 2. Female.

Lith. Printed & Col.d by J.T.Bowen, Phil.a

Pl. 344.

Yellow Shanks Snipe.
Male. Summer Plumage.
View in South Carolina.

Drawn from Nature by J.J. Audubon F.R.S.F.L.S.

Lith.d Printed & Col.d by J.T Bowen, Philad.a

Pl. 345.

Drawn from Nature by J.J.Audubon, F.R.S.F.L.S.

Tell-tale Godwit or Snipe.
1 Male. 2 Female.
View of East Florida.

Lith⁴ Printed & Col⁴ by J. T. Bowen Philad⁴.

Pl. 346.

Greenshank.

Male.

View of St. Augustine & Spanish Fort East Florida.

Drawn from Nature by J.J.Audubon,F.R.S.F.L.S.

Lith⁴ Printed & Col⁴ by J T Bowen Phil.ad⁴

Pl 347.

Semipalmated Snipe. Willet or Stone Curlew.

1. Male Spring Plumage. 2. Female in Winter.

Drawn from Nature by J.J.Audubon, F.R.S.F.L.S.

Lith.Printed & Col.d by J T Bowen Phil.ad.

355

Pl. 348.

Great Marbled Godwit.

1. Male. 2. Female.

Drawn from Nature by J.J.Audubon,F.R.S.F.L.S.

Lith\`d Printed & Col\`d by J.T. Bowen, Philad\`a

Pl. 349.

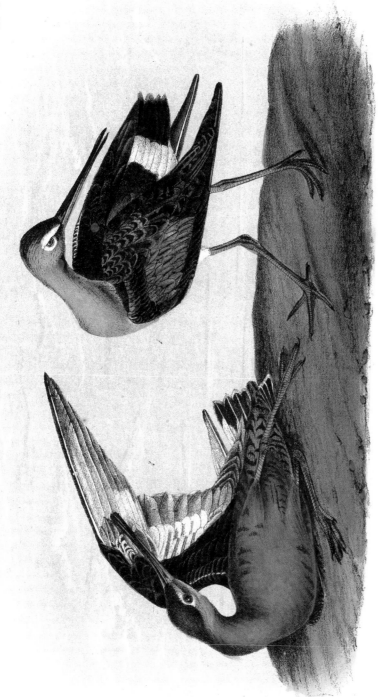

Drawn from Nature by J.J.Audubon,FRSFLS.

Hudsonian Godwit.

1. Male, 2, Female Summer Plumage.

Lith Printed & Col ᵈ by J T Bowen, Phil ᵃ ᵈ ᵃ

Pl 350

Wilson's Snipe – Common Snipe.
Plantation near Charleston, S.C.

Drawn from Nature by J.J Audubon, F.R.S.F.L.S

Bowen & Co lith & col. Philada.

Pl 351

Drawn from Nature by J.J.Audubon.FRSFLS.

Red-breasted Snipe

1. Spring Plumage 2. Winter.

Lith.d Printed & Col.d by J T Bowen Philad.

Pl. 352.

American Woodcock

1. Male. 2. Female. 3. Young in Autumn.

Drawn from Nature by J.J.Audubon, FRS.FLS.

Lith.d Printed & Col.d by J.T.Bowen, Philad.a

360

Pl. 353.

American Avocet

Young in first Winter Plumage Adult in the Distance.

Drawn from Nature by J.J.Audubon.F.R.S.F.L.S.

Lith⁴ Printed & Col⁴ by J.T.Bowen Philad⁴

Pl. 354.

Black Necked Stilt.

Male.

Pl. 355.

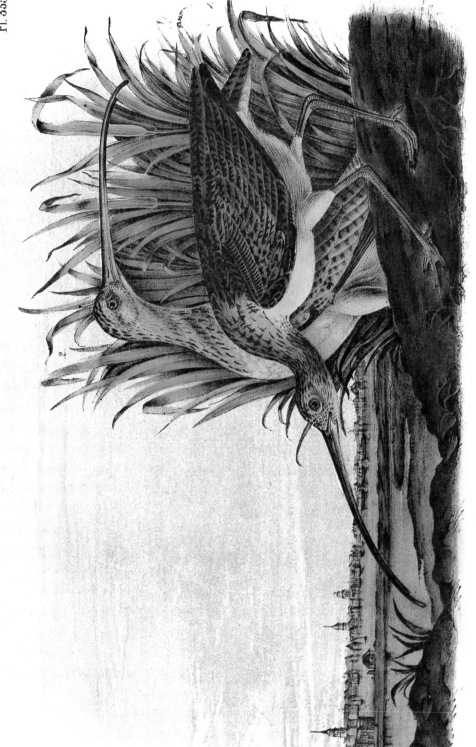

Long-billed Curlew
1. Male. 2. Female.
City of Charleston.

Drawn from Nature by J.J.Audubon,FRSFLS.

Lith⁴.Printed & Col⁴.by J. T.Bowen, Philad

363

Pl. 356

Lith'd Printed & Col'd by J.T.Bowen. Philad'a

Hudsonian Curlew
Male.

Drawn from Nature by J.J.Audubon.FRS.FLS.

Pl. 357

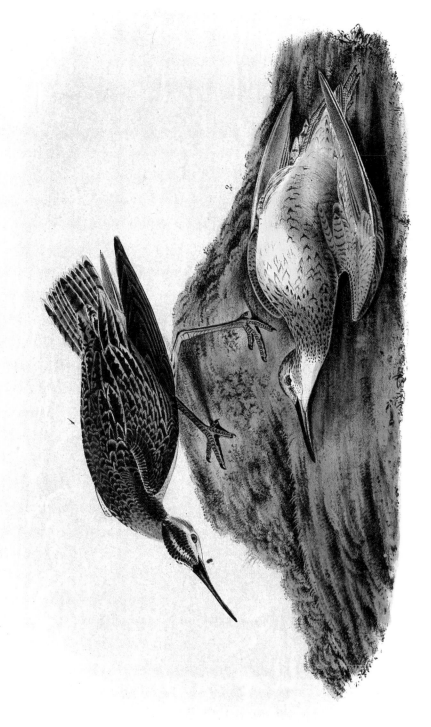

Esquimaux Curlew.
1. Male. 2. Female.

Drawn from Nature by J.J.Audubon, F.R.S.F.L.S.

Lithd Printed & Cold by J.T.Bowen Philada

Pl. 358.

Glossy Ibis.
Adult Male.

Drawn from Nature by J.J.Audubon,F.R.S.F.L.S.

Lith.dPrinted & Col.d by J.T.Bowen, Philad.a

Pl. 359.

Scarlet Ibis.

1. Adult male. 2. Young second Autumn.

Drawn from Nature by J.J.Audubon.F.R.S.F.L.S.

Lith. Printed & Col.d by J.T.Bowen, Philad.a

Pl. 360.

Lith'Printed & Col'd by J.T.Bowen Philad.ª

White Ibis.

1. Adult. 2. Young in Autumn.

Drawn from Nature by J.J.Audubon. F.R.S.F.L.S.

368

Pl. 361.

Wood Ibis.

Male.

Drawn from Nature by J.J.Audubon, F.R.S.F.L.S.   Lith⁴ Printed & Col⁴ by J. T. Bowen, Philad⁴

Roseate Spoonbill
Male.

Drawn from Nature by J.J.Audubon.FRS.FLS.

Lith.d Printed & Col.d by J.T.Bowen, Philad.a

Black-Crowned Night Heron or Qua Bird.

1 Adult. 2. Young.

Drawn from Nature by J.J Audubon, F.R.S.FL.

Lith. Printed & Col.d by J.T Bowen, Philad.

Pl. 364

Yellow Crowned Night Heron.

1 Adult Male, Spring Plumage 2 Young in October.

Drawn from Nature by J.J.Audubon,F.R.S.F.L.S.

Lith^d Printed & Col^d by J. T. Bowen, Philad^a.

Pl. 365.

American Bittern.

1. Male. 2. Female.

Drawn from Nature by J.J.Audubon, F.R.S.F.L.S.

Lith.d Printed & Col.d by J. T. Bowen Phila.d

Pl. 366

Least Bittern.

1. Male. 2. Female. 3 Young.

Pl. 367

Green Heron.
1 Adult Male. 2 Young in Sept.

Drawn from Nature by J.J.Audubon.FRS.FLS

Lith.d Printed & Col.d by J. T Bowen Philad.a

Pl. 366

Drawn from Nature by J.J.Audubon.F.R.S.F.L.S.

Great White Heron.
. *Male adult . Spring Plumage .*

Lithᵈ Printed & Colᵈ by J T Bowen. Philadᵃ

Pl. 369

Great blue Heron.

Male.

Drawn from Nature by J.J.Audubon,F.R.S.F.L.S.

Lith.d Printed & Col.d by J.T.Bowen, Philad.a

Pl. 370

Great American White Egret.
Male. Spring plumage.

Drawn from Nature by J.J. Audubon.FR.S.FL.S

Lith & Col.d by Bowen & Co. Philad.a

Reddish. Egret

1 Adult, full Spring Plumage. 2. Young in full Spring Plumage two Years old

Drawn from Nature by J.J Audubon F.R.S F.L.S.

Lith & Col. by Bowen & C.º Philad.ª

Pl. 372

Blue Heron

Drawn from Nature by J.J.Audubon,F.R.S.F.L.S.

1. Male adult Spring Plumage 2. Young 3rd ~~ ~ ..

Lith Printed & Col.d by J T Bowen Philad.a

Pl. 373

Drawn from Nature by J.J.Audubon.FRSFLS.

Lithᵈ Printed & Colᵈ by J.T.Bowen, Philadᵃ

Louisiana Heron.

Male Adult.

381

Pl. 374

Snowy Heron.

Drawn from Nature by J.J.Audubon, F.R.S.E.L.S.   *Male*   Lith.& Col.d by Bowen & Co, Philada.

American Flamingo

Drawn from Nature by J.J. Audubon.F.R.S.FLS

Adult. Male

383

Lith & Col.Bowen & C° Philad.ª

Pl. 376.

Canada Goose.

1. Male 2. Female.

Drawn from Nature by J.J.Audubon,FRSFLS.

Lith.d Printed & Col.d by J.T.Bowen, Philad.a

Pl. 377.

Hutchins's Goose!

Adule Male.

Drawn from Nature by J.J.Audubon,F.R.S.F.L.S.

Lith⁴ Printed & Col⁴by J.T.Bowen, Philad⁴

Pl. 378

Bernacle Goose

1. Male 2. Female.

Drawn from Nature by J.J.Audubon.FRS.FLS.

Lith'.Printed & Col'.by J.T.Bowen, Philad'.

Pl. 379.

Brant Goose

1. Male 2. Female.

Drawn from Nature by J.J.Audubon, F.R.S.F.L.S.

Lith.⁴ Printed & Col.⁴ by J.T.Bowen, Philad.ᵃ

Pl. 380.

White-fronted Goose.
1. Male. 2. Female.

Drawn from Nature by J.J.Audubon,FRSFLS.

Lith.d Printed & Col.d by J. T. Bowen. Phila.d

Pl. 381

Snow Goose

Adult male. Young female.

Drawn from Nature by J.J.Audubon.F.R.S.F.L.S.

Lith⁴ Printed & Col⁴ by J. T. Bowen Philad⁻

Pl. 382.

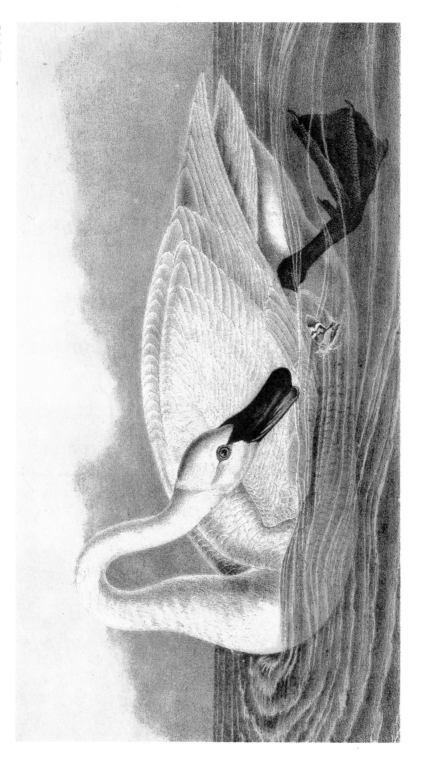

Drawn from Nature by J.J.Audubon.FRSFLS.

Trumpeter Swan
Adult.

Lith.d Printed & Col.d by J T.Bowen, Philad.a

Pl. 383.

Drawn from Nature by J.J.Audubon,F.R.S.F.L.S.

Trumpeter Swan.

Young.

Lith⁴ Printed & Col⁴ by J T Bowen, Philad⁴

Pl. 384.

American Swan

Male.

Drawn from Nature by J.J.Audubon,FRSFLS.

Lith⁴ Printed & Col⁴ by J.T.Bowen Philad⁴

Pl. 385.

Mallard

1. 2. *Males. 3. 4. Females.*

Drawn from Nature by J.J.Audubon, F.R.S.F.L.S.

Lith. Printed & Col.d by J T.Bowen, Philad.a

Pl. 386

Drawn from Nature by J.J.Audubon.FRS.FLS.

Dusky Duck.
1. Male. 2. Female.

Lith.d Printed & Col.d by J. T Bowen, Philad.a

Pl. 387.

Drawn from Nature by J.J.Audubon,F.R.S.F.L.S.

R.T.

Brewers Duck.

Male.

Lith.Printed & Col.d by J.T Bowen,Philad.a

395

Pl. 388.

Drawn from Nature by J.J.Audubon.F.R.S.F.L.S.

Gadwall Duck.

1. Male. 2. Female.

Lith.d Printed & Col.d by J. T. Bowen, Phila.d.

396

Pl. 389.

American Widgeon.
1. Male 2. Female.

Drawn from Nature by J.J.Audubon.F.R.S.F.L.S.

Lith.d Printed & Col.d by J.T.Bowen, Philad.a

397

Pl. 390

Lith⁴ Printed & Col⁴ by J. T Bowen, Philad⁴

Pintail Duck.

1. *Male.* 2. *Female.*

Drawn from Nature by J.J.Audubon.F.R.S.F.L.S.

Pl. 391

Wood Duck Summer Duck

1 Male 2 Female

Drawn from Nature by J.J Audubon FRSFLS

Lith* Printed & Col* by J.T.Bowen, Philad*

Pl. 392

Drawn from Nature by J.J.Audubon.FRS.FLS

American Green - winged Teal

1Male 2 Females.

Lith?Printed & Col?by J.T.Bowen. Philad?

Pl. 343.

Drawn from Nature by J.J.Audubon.FRS.FLS

Litho Printed & Col'd by J. T. Bowen, Philad'a

Blue-winged Teal.

1. Male. 2. Female.

Pl. 394

Drawn from Nature by J.J Audubon, F.R.S.F.L.S.

Lith. Printed & Colᵈ by J.T.Bowen, Philᵃ

Shoveller Duck.

1 Male 2 Female.

402

Pl. 395

Canvass Back Duck
1 Male 2 Female.
VIEW OF BALTIMORE, MARYLAND

Drawn from Nature by J.J.Audubon,FRSFLS

Lith.d Printed & Col.d by J T Bowen, Philad.a

Pl. 396

Red-headed Duck.

1. Male. 2. Female.

404

Pl. 397.

Scaup Duck.

1 Male. 2. Female.

Drawn from Nature by J.J.Audubon, F.R.S.F.L.S.

LithPrinted & Col^d by J.T.Bowen, Philad^a

Pl. 398.

Drawn from Nature by J.J.Audubon,F.R.S.F.L.S.

Ring-necked Duck.
1. Male. 2. Female.

Lith.d Printed & Col.d by J T Bowen, Phil.da

Pl. 399.

Ruddy Duck.

1. Male. 2. Female. 3. Young.

Drawn from Nature by J.J. Audubon. F.R.S.F.L.S.

Lith Printed & Col^d by J.T. Bowen Philad^a

Pl. 400

Pied Duck.

1. Male. 2. Female.

Drawn from Nature by J.J.Audubon.FRS.FLS.

Lith.d Printed & Col.d by J T Bowen Philad.a

Pl. 401.

Velvet Duck

1. Male. 2. Female.

Drawn from Nature by J.J.Audubon.FRSFLS.

Lith.d Printed & Col.d by J. T. Bowen. Philad.a

Pl. 402.

Black or Surf Duck

Drawn from Nature by J.J Audubon FRS.FLS

1. Male 2. Female

Lith d Printed & Col d by J.T Bowen Philad a

Pl. 403.

American Scoter Duck

1. Male. 2. Female

Drawn from Nature by J J Audubon FRSFLS

Lith: Printed & Col:d by J T Bowen, Philad:a

Pl. 404

King Duck.
1 *Male. 2 Female.*

Drawn from Nature by J.J. Audubon, F.R.S.F.L.S.

Lith.Printed & Col.d by J.T.Bowen, Philad.a

Pl. 405

Eider Duck

1. Male 2. Female.

Pl 406

Golden Eye Duck.

1 Male   2 Female

Drawn from Nature by J.J.Audubon, FRS.FLS

Lith.Printed & Col.d by J T Bowen Philad.a

Pl. 407.

Western Duck

Male.

Drawn from Nature by J.J.Audubon, FRSFLS.

Lith.Printed & Col.d by J T Bowen. Phila.d

415

Pl. 408

Drawn from Nature by J.J.Audubon,F.R.S.F.L.S

Buffel headed - Duck

1. Male. 2. Female.

Lith⁴Printed & Col⁴by J T Bowen, Philad⁴

Pl. 409.

Drawn from Nature by J.J.Audubon,FRSFLS

Lith?Printed & Col?hy J. T. Bowen, Philad?

Harlequin Duck.
1. old. Male, 2. Female 3 Young Male.

Pl 410.

Long-tailed Duck

1. Male. Summer Plumage. 2. Male in Winter. 3. Female and Young.

Drawn from Nature by J.J.Audubon, F.R.S.F.L.S.

Lith:Printed & Col:dby J T Bowen Philad:a

Pl. 411.

Buff-breasted Merganter. Goosander.

1. Male. 2. Female.

Drawn from Nature by J.J.Audubon,FRS.FLS.

Lith.d Printed & Col.d by J.T.Bowen, Philad.a

Pl. 412.

Red-breasted Merganser.

1. Male. 2. Female.

Drawn from Nature by J.J.Audubon.F.R.S.F.L.S.

Lith.d Printed & Col.d by J.T.Bowen. Philad.a

Pl. 413.

Drawn from Nature by J.J.Audubon.F.R.S.F.L.S.

Hooded Merganser.

1. Male. 2. Female.

Lith.Printed & Col.d by J. T. Bowen Philad.

Pl. 414.

White Merganser, Smew, White Nun.

1. Male. 2. Female.

Drawn from Nature by J.J.Audubon,F.R.S.F.L.S.

Bowen & Co. lith.& col. Philada.

Pl. 415.

Drawn from Nature by J.J.Audubon.FRSFLS.

Common Cormorant

1. Male. 2. Female 3 Young.

Lith.d Printed & Col.d by J T Bowen, Philad.

Pl. 416.

Double-crested-Cormorant.

Male.

Drawn from Nature by J.J.Audubon.FRS.FLS.

Lith^d.Printed & Col^dby J.T.Bowen Philad^a

Pl. 417

Drawn from Nature by J.J.Audubon.FRS.F.L.S.

Florida Cormorant

Male.

Lith.d Printed & Col.d by J.T.Bowen Philad.a

425

Townsend's Cormorant

Male.

Drawn from Nature by J.J.Audubon,FRSFLS Lith.d Printed & Col.d by J.T Bowen Philad.a

426

Pl. 419.

Violet-green Cormorant.

Female in Winter.

Drawn from Nature by J.J.Audubon,FRS.FLS.

Lith⁴ Printed & Col⁴ by J.T.Bowen, Philad⁴

Pl. 420.

American Anhinga Snake Bird.

1. Male. 2. Female.

Drawn from Nature by J.J.Audubon,F.R.S.F.L.S

Lith⁴ Printed & Col⁴ by J. T. Bowen, Philad⁴

Pl. 421.

Frigate Pelican Man of War bird.

Male.

Drawn from Nature by J.J.Audubon,F.R.S.F.L.S.

Lith⁴Printed & Col⁴by J. T. Bowen, Philad⁴

Pl. 422.

W.H.

American White Pelican.

Male.

Drawn from Nature by J.J.Audubon,FRS.FLS. Lith.ᵈPrinted & Col.ᵈby J. T. Bowen, Philad.ᵃ

Pl 423.

Brown Pelican

Adult Male.

Drawn from Nature by J.J.Audubon,F.R.S.F.L.S

Lith'Printed & Col'by J T Bowen, Philad:

Pl 424.

Brown Pelican

Young first Winter.

Drawn from Nature by J.J.Audubon.F.R.S.F.L.S.

Lith⁴ Printed & Col⁴ by J.T.Bowen. Philad.ª

Pl 425

Common Gannet.

1. Adult male. 2. Young.

Drawn from Nature by J.J.Audubon,F.R.S.F.L.S.

Lith.d Printed & Col.d by J T.Bowen,Philad.a

Pl. 426.

Booby Gannet.

Male.

Drawn from Nature by J.J.Audubon, F.R.S.F.L.S.

Lith.d Printed & Col.d by J. T. Bowen, Philad.a

Pl 427

Drawn from Nature by J.J.Audubon.F.R.S.F.L.S.

Tropic Bird.
1 Male 2 Female

Lith⁴ Printed & Col⁴ by J. T. Bowen, Phila⁴⁴

435

Pl. 428.

Drawn from Nature by J.J.Audubon.F.R.S.F.L.S.

Black Skimmer or Shearwater.
Male.

Lith:d Printed & Col:d by J. T Bowen, Philad:a

Pl. 429.

Cayenne Tern.

Drawn from Nature by J.J.Audubon, FRSFLS.

Lith.d Printed & Col.d by J.T.Bowen, Philad.a

Pl. 430.

Gull-billed Tern – Marsh Tern.

Male.

Drawn from Nature by J.J.Audubon,F.R.S.F.L.S.   Lith.ᵈ Printed & Col.ᵈ by J. T. Bowen, Philad.ᵃ

Drawn from Nature by J J Audubon FRS FLS

Sandwich Tern.

Adult

Lith & Col by Bowen & Cᵒ Phiada

439

Pl. 432.

Drawn from Nature by J.J.Audubon.FRSFLS.

Sooty Tern

Lith.Printed & Col.d by J T Bowen,Philad:

Pl 433.

Common Tern.

Male Spring Plumage.

Drawn from Nature by J.J.Audubon.FRS.FLS.   Lith? Printed & Col? by J.T.Bowen, Philad?

Pl. 434.

Havell's Tern.

Adult.

Pl. 435.

Trudeau's Tern.

Adult.

Drawn from Nature by J.J.Audubon.F.R.S.F.L.S.

Lith⁴ Printed & Col⁴ by J.T.Bowen Philad⁴

Drawn from nature by J. W. Audubon.   Lith. & col. by Bowen & Co. Philad.ᵃ

Arctic Tern
444

Pl. 437

Light House, St. John, New Brunswick.

Roseate Tern.

Male

Drawn from Nature by J.J.Audubon, F.R.S.F.L.S.   Lith & Col.d by Bowen & Co. Philad.a

445

Pl. 438

Black Tern.

1. Adult. 2. Young.

Drawn from Nature by J.J.Audubon,F.R.S.F.L.S.   Lith.d Printed & Col.d by J.T.Bowen, Philad.a

446

Pl. 439.

Least Tern.

1. Adult in Spring 2. Young.

Drawn from Nature by J.J.Audubon,F.R.S.F.L.S.   Lith⁴Printed & Col⁴by J T Bowen, Philad⁴

Pl. 440.

Noddy Tern.
Male.

Drawn from Nature by J.J.Audubon.FRSFLS

Lith.Printed & Col.d by J.T.H....

Pl. 441.

Fork-tailed Gull

Male.

Drawn from Nature by J.J.Audubon.FRS.FLS.

Lith.Printed & Col.d by J.T.Bowen,Philad.a

Pl. 442.

Bonapartes Gull

1. Male in Spring. - 2. Female. - 3. Young First Autumn.

Drawn from Nature by J.J.Audubon. F.R.S.F.L.S.

Lith⁴ Printed & Col⁴ by J.T.Bowen. Philad⁴.

Pl. 443

Drawn from Nature by J.J.Audubon,F.R.S.F.L.S.

Lith⁴ Printed & Col⁴ by J.T.Bowen, Philad⁴

Black-headed Gull.

1. Adult Male Spring Plumage. 2. Young First Autumn.

Pl 444.

Drawn from Nature by J.J.Audubon.FRSFLS.

Kittiwake Gull.

1 Adult - 2. Young.

Lith.d Printed & Col.d by J T Bowen Philad.a

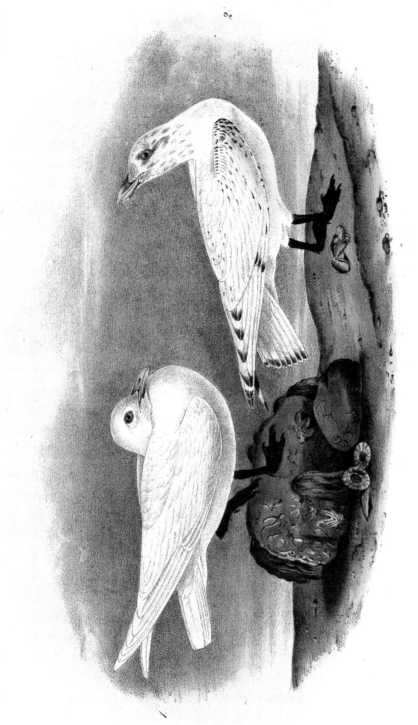

Pl. 445

Ivory Gull.
1.Adult Male. 2.Young second Autumn.

Drawn from Nature by J.J.Audubon.F.R.S.F.L.S.

Lith.Printed & Col.d by J.T.Bowen, Phil.d.

453

Pl. 446

Common American Gull... Ring-billed Gull.
(Adult 2 Young.)

Drawn from Nature by J.J.Audubon.FRSFLS.

Lith.ᵈPrinted & Col.ᵈby J.T.Bowen.Philad.ᵈ

454

Pl. 447.

White winged Silvery Gull.

1. Male in Summer. 2. Young in Winter.

Drawn from Nature by J.J. Audubon, FRS.FLS

Lith⁴ Printed & Col⁴ by J T Bowen, Phil.ad.

Pl. 448.

Herring or Silvery Gull

1. Adult in Spring. 2. Young in Autumn.

Drawn from Nature by J.J.Audubon FRSFLS　　　　　　　Lith⁴ Printed & Col⁴ by J.T.Bowen Philad.

Pl 449

2

Glaucus Gull. Burgomaster.

Adult male & Young First Autumn.

Drawn from Nature by J.J.Audubon,FRS.FLS

Lith⁴ Printed & Col⁴ by J.T.Bowen Phila.ᵈ

Pl. 450.

WEH

Great Black backed Gull.

Male.

Drawn from Nature by J.J.Audubon,FRSFLS.   Lith.ᵈ Printed & Col.ᵈ by J.T.Bowen, Philad.ᵃ

Pl. 451.

Pomerine Jager.
Adult Female.

Drawn from Nature by J.J. Audubon. F.R.S.F.L.S.

Lith⁴ Printed & Col⁴ by J.T. Bowen, Philad.ᵃ

Pl. 452.

Drawn from Nature by J.J.Audubon. FRS.Fl.S.

Richardson Jager

1. Male Adult. 2. Young in Septr.

Lith⁴Printed & Col⁴by J T Bowen, Philad⁴

Pl. 453

Arctic Jager.

Drawn from Nature by J.J.Audubon,FRSFLS. Lith⁴Printed & Col⁴by J. T. Bowen, Philad⁴

Pl. 454.

Drawn from Nature by J.J.Audubon.F.R.S.F.L.S.

Dusky Albatros

Lith.d Printed & Col.d by J.T.Bowen. Philad.a

Pl. 455.

N.F.11.

Fulmar Petrel

Adult Male Summer Plumage.

Drawn from Nature by J.J.Audubon.F.R.S.F.L.S.

Lith.Printed & Col.d by J.T.Bowen Philad.a

Pl. 456.

Drawn from Nature by J.J.Audubon.F.R.S.F.L.S.

Wandering Shearwater.
Male.

Lith^d Printed & Col^d by J T Bowen Philad^a

Pl. 467.

Manks Shearwater.

Male.

Drawn from Nature by J.J.Audubon. F.R.S.F.L.S.

Lith. Printed & Col.d by J.T. Bowen Philad.a

Pl. 458.

Dusky Shearwater.
Male in Spring.

Drawn from Nature by J.J.Audubon.F.R.S.F.L.S.

Lith⁴Printed & Col⁴ by J.T.Bowen.Philad⁴

466

Pl. 459.

Leach's Petrel.– Forked-tailed Petrel.

1. Male. 2. Female.

Drawn from Nature by J.J.Audubon.FRSFLS.

Lith⁴Printed & Col⁴by. J T Bowen, Philad⁴.

Pl. 460.

Wilson's Petrel. Mother Carey's chicken.

1. Male. 2. Female

Drawn from Nature by J.J.Audubon.F.R.S.F.L.s.

Lith. Printed & Col. by J T Bowen. Philad.a

Pl. 461.

Drawn from Nature by J.J.Audubon F.R.S.FL.S.

Least Petrel – Mother Carey's chicken!

1. Male. 2. Female.

Lith⁴ Printed & Col⁴ by J T Bowen Philad⁴

Pl. 462.

Tufted Puffin.
1. Male. 2. Female.

Drawn from Nature by J.J. Audubon FRS FLS

Lith.d Printed & Col.d by J.T. Bowen, Philad.a

Pl. 463.

Drawn from Nature by J.J.Audubon,F.R.S.F.L.S.

Large billed Puffin.

1. Male. 2. Female.

Lith⁴ Printed & Col⁴ by J T Bowen, Philad⁴

Pl. 464.

Drawn from Nature by J.J.Audubon,F.R.S.F.L.S.

Common or Arctic Puffin.
1. Male. 2. Female.

Lith.Printed & Col.d by J T Bowen, Philad.a

Plate 465

Great Auk

Adult.

Drawn from Nature by J.J. Audubon, F.R.S.F.L.S.

Lith. Printed & Col.d by J.T. Bowen, Phila.d

Plate 466

Drawn from Nature by J.J Audubon,F.R.S.F.L.S.

Razor-billed Auk
1 Male. 2 Female

Lith⁹ Printed & Col⁴ by J T Bowen, Philad⁴

Pl. 467.

Curled-crested Phaleris.

Adult.

Drawn from Nature by J.J.Audubon.FRS.FLS.

Lith.Printed & Col.d by J.T Bowen.Philad.d

Pl. 468.

Knobbed-billed Phaleris.

Adult.

Drawn from Nature by J.J.Audubon.FRS.FLS.

Lith. Printed & Col.d by J.T.Bowen. Philad.a

476

Pl. 469.

Little Auk - Sea dove

1. Male. 2. Female.

Drawn from Nature by J.J.Audubon.FRSFLS.

Lith⁴ Printed & Col⁴ by J T Bowen, Philad⁴

Pl 470

Black throated Guillemot

Adult 2 Young

Drawn from Nature by J J Audubon FRS FLS

Lith. Printed & Col.d by J T Bowen, Philad.

Pl. 411.

Horned-billed Guillemot

Adult.

Drawn from Nature by J.J.Audubon.FRS.FLS

Lith.Printed & Col.d by J.T.Bowen. Philad.a

Pl. 472.

Drawn from Nature by J.J.Audubon,F.R.S.F.L.S.

Large-billed Guillemot.

Male.

Pl. 473.

Drawn from Nature by J.J.Audubon.FRS.FLS

Foolish Guillemot. Murre.

1. Male. 2. Female.

Lith.d Printed & Col.d by J.T.Bowen Phila.d

Pl. 474

Black Guillimot.

1. Adult - Summer Plumage - 2. Adult in Winter - 3. Young.

Drawn from Nature by J.J.Audubon.FRSFLS   Lith.Printed & Col.d by J T Bowen Philad.a

Pl. 475.

Slender-billed Guillemot.

1. Male. 2. Female.

Drawn from Nature by J.J. Audubon, F.R.S.F.L.S.

Lith? Printed & Col? by J T Bowen Philad?

483

Pl. 476

Great North Diver — Loon.
1 Adult 2 Young in Winter

Drawn from Nature by J.J.Audubon,FRS.FLS.

Lith\.Printed & Col\.d by J.T.Bowen, Philad\.a

484

Pl. 477.

Black-throated Diver.

1. Male. 2. Female 3. Young in Oder.

Drawn from Nature by J.J.Audubon.F.R.S.F.L.S.

Lith Printed & Col.d by J.T Bowen Phil.d.

485

Pl. 478.

Red-throated Diver.

1. Male Summer Plumage 2. do. Winter 3 Female. 4. Young

Drawn from Nature by J.J. Audubon FRSFLS.

Lith Printed & Col d by J T Bowen Philad a

Pl. 479

Crested Grebe.

1. Adult Male in Spring 2 Young (first Winter.)

Drawn from Nature by J J Audubon. F R S F L S.

Lith.d Printed & Col.d by J T Bowen, Phila.d

Pl. 480

Red-necked Grebe.
1. Adult Male Spring Plumage 2. Young Winter Plumage.

Drawn from Nature by J.J. Audubon. FRS.FLS.

Lith. Printed & Col.d by J. T. Bowen Philad.a

Pl. 481

Horned Grebe

1 Adult Male. 2 Female in Winter

Drawn from Nature by J.J.Audubon F.R.S.F.L.S.

Lith.ᵈ Printed & Col.ᵈ by J. T.Bowen Philad.ᵃ

Pl. 482

Drawn from Nature by J.J.Audubon F.R.S.F.L.S.

Lith Printed & Col^d By J.T.Bowen Philad^a

Eared Grebe
1. Male 2 Young first Year.

490

Pl. 483.

Drawn from Nature by J.J.Audubon.F.R.S.F.L.S.

Pied-billed Dotchick.

1. Male. 2. Female.

Pl 484.

WEH

Harris' Finch.

1. Adult Male 2. Young Female.

Drawn from Nature by J.J.Audubon,FRSFLS.

Lith⁴Printed & Col⁴by J T Bowen, Philad⁴

Pl. 485

Bell's Vireo.
Male
Rattle-snake Root.

Drawn from Nature by J.J.Audubon,F.R.S.F.L.S.

Lith.d Printed & Col.d by J.T.Bowen, Philad:

493

Pl. 486.

Sprague's Missouri Lark.

Male.

Drawn from Nature by J.J.Audubon.FRS.FLS.

Lith.Printed & Col.d by J.T.Bowen Philad.a

Drawn from Nature by J.J.Audubon,F.R.S.F.L.S.

Smith's Lark Bunting?

Adult Male

Lith^d Printed & Col^d by J. T. Bowen. Philad^a.

Pl. 488.

Le Contis Sharp-tailed Bunting.

Male.

Drawn from Nature by J.J.Audubon,FRSFLS.   Lith. Printed & Col. by J. T. Bowen, Philad.

Pl. 489

Missouri Meadow Lark?

Male.

Drawn from Nature by J.J.Audubon,FRSFLS.

Lith⁴ Printed & Col⁴ by J. T. Bowen, Phil⁴

Pl. 490.

Yellow-bellied Flycatcher.

Male.

Drawn from Nature by J.J.Audubon,FRSFLS. 498 Lith.d Printed & Col.d by J.T.Bowen, Philad.a

Pl. 491.

Least Flycatcher.

Male.

Drawn from Nature by J.J.Audubon,FRSFLS.   Lith⁴Printed & Col⁴by J.T.Bowen Philad⁴

Pl. 492.

Brewers Black bird

Male.

Drawn from Nature by J.J.Audubon,F.R.S.F.L.S.

Lith⁴ Printed & Col⁴ by J.T.Bowen, Philad⁴

Pl. 493.

Shattucks Bunting?

Male.

Drawn from Nature by J.J.Audubon,F.R.S.F.L.S.

Lith⁴Printed & Col⁴by J.T.Bowen,Philad⁴

501

Pl. 494

Missouri Red-moustached Woodpecker.

Male.

Drawn from Nature by J.J.Audubon FRS.FLS   Lith⁴ Printed & Col⁴ by J T Bowen, Philad⁴

502

Pl. 495

Drawn from Nature by J.J.Audubon.FRSFLS.

Nuttall's Whip-poor-will.

Male.

Lith.d Printed & Col.d by J T Bowen Philad.a

Pl. 496.

The Texan Turtle Dove.

Male.

Drawn from Nature by J.J.Audubon,FRSFLS.

Lith^dPrinted & Col^dby J T Bowen Philad^a

Pl 497

Drawn from Nature by J.J.Audubon F.R.S.F.L.S.

Western Shore Lark.

Male.

Lith⁴ Printed & Col⁴ by J T Bowen. Philad⁴

505

Pl. 498.

Drawn from Nature by J.J.Audubon,FRSFLS.

Common Scaup Duck?

1. Male. 2. Female.

Lith'd Printed & Col'd by J T Bowen Philad'

Pl 499.

Common Troupial.

Male.

Drawn from Nature by J.J.Audubon.FRSFLS.   Lith⁴ Printed & Col⁴ by J T Bowen, Philad⁴

Pl. 500

Baird's Bunting.

Male.

Drawn from Nature by J.J.Audubon, F.R.S.F.L.S.

LithPrinted & Col^d by J.T.Bowen, Philad^a

Index in Order of Appearance

510

511